ALTIERO SPINELLI AND THE BRITISH FEDERALISTS

Writings by Beveridge, Robbins and Spinelli 1937-1943

Edited and Introduced by
John Pinder

FEDERALTRUST

THE FEDERAL TRUST

The Federal Trust undertakes research and education on the application of federal principles within the United Kingdom, the European Union and the wider world. It focuses in particular on the widening and deepening of the European Union and on Britain's European policy.

The Trust conducts enquiries, promotes seminars and conferences and publishes reports and teaching materials on these themes.

It is the UK member of TEPSA (the Trans-European Policy Studies Association).

Up-to-date information about the Federal Trust can be found on the internet at www.fedtrust.co.uk.

The Federal Trust is a registered charity and expresses no political view of its own.

Published by the Federal Trust
Dean Bradley House
52 Horseferry Road
London SW1P 2AF
© Federal Trust for Education and Research 1998
ISBN 0 901573 58 2
The Federal Trust is a Registered Charity
Marketing and Distribution by Kogan Page Ltd
Printed in the European Union

ALTIERO SPINELLI AND THE BRITISH FEDERALISTS:
WRITINGS BY BEVERIDGE, ROBBINS AND SPINELLI
1937-1943

Contents

PREFACE vii

INTRODUCTION by John Pinder 1

BEVERIDGE'S PROPOSAL FOR A FEDERAL EUROPE
Introductory note 17
Peace by Federation?, by Sir William Beveridge 19

ROBBINS: A FEDERAL FRAMEWORK FOR AN INTERNATIONAL
ECONOMY
Introductory note 45
'A federal government for a liberal international
economy', extract from *Economic Planning and
International Order*, by Lionel Robbins 49
'The need for a European federation', extract from *The
Economic Causes of War*, by Lionel Robbins 61

SPINELLI ON VENTOTENE
Introductory note 69
The Ventotene Manifesto, by Altiero Spinelli and
Ernesto Rossi 73
'The United States of Europe and the Various Political
Tendencies', by Altiero Spinelli 87

FURTHER READING 121

NOTES 127

INDEX 137

Acknowledgments

The Federal Trust is most grateful to the Altiero Spinelli Institute for Federalist Studies for supplying English translations of the Ventotene Manifesto and of Spinelli's essay on 'The United States of Europe and the Various Political Tendencies', as well as to the Institute and, above all, to Franco Spoltore for their encouragement to undertake this work. The author's thanks are due to the Federal Trust's Director, Andrew Duff, for his wise advice and also to Owen Burdekin and Judy Keep for helping to get the book into a form that is fit to print.

About the Author

John Pinder is the Chairman of the Federal Trust and a Visiting Professor at the College of Europe. He was International Director of the Economist Intelligence Unit until 1964, then Director of the Policy Studies Institute (formerly Political and Economic Planning) until 1985. He is a Vice President of the international European Movement, former Deputy Chairman of the European Movement, UK, and Honorary President of the Union of European Federalists. His publications include *Federal Union: The Pioneers - A History of Federal Union* (with Richard Mayne, 1990), *The European Community and Eastern Europe* (1991), *Maastricht and Beyond* (co-editor and co-author, 1994), *European Unity and World Order - Federal Trust 1945-1995* (1995), *The Building of the European Union* (3rd edn, 1998; 1st edn, 1991), and *Foundations of Democracy in the European Union* (1999, forthcoming).

Preface

In 1950, when I found the British federalist literature of the period to which the writings reproduced in this book belong, I was struck by its quality and convinced by its message. The quality of the writings reflected that of the authors, who included academics such as Ivor Jennings, Harold Laski, Lionel Robbins, Arnold Toynbee and Kenneth Wheare, as well as those with a political vocation such as Lord Lothian, Barbara Wootton and Kim Mackay. The logic of the message, after the experience of World War Two, was ineluctable. A democratic federal government to manage their common affairs would be the best guarantee that the member states would not go to war with each other again, while leaving their several democratic governments free to order their own domestic affairs.

The European Community, now the Union, has indeed done much to make peace, for the first time in history, the normal condition throughout Western Europe, with the prospect that it will before long be enlarged to include most of Central and Eastern Europe too; and this has been achieved through the incremental application of federal principles to the management of important sectors of the member states' common affairs. It has not been done, however, by the direct approach that these British federalists envisaged, of placing the armed forces under federal control. As the failure in the mid-1950s of the project of the European Defence Community showed, this was politically too sensitive to secure wide enough acceptance. But the common affairs to which the federal principle applied were not confined to the military aspects of security. The interdependence among states that is the basis for the federal project was growing ever more intense in the fields of the economy and the environment; and it is here that the federalist approach has been successfully applied. The acceptance of a common rule of law throughout the member states, and hence of common institutions for legislation and for execution of the law, has replaced relations based on power for a substantial part of their mutual relationship. In a way that the earlier British federalists did not foresee, this incremental approach, of which Jean Monnet was the pioneer, has gone far towards achieving their fundamental aim, even though the Union's institutions still need to be made more effective and more democratic.

Because the fortunes of war favoured the British, this literature of the 1930s and early 1940s has been forgotten in Britain and its message that sovereignty should be shared has been resisted. For many of our Continental neighbours, to the contrary, the fruits of national sovereignty had tasted very bitter and they were attracted by the federal idea. So the belief grew among the British that this was a Continental invention. It is surely hard to credit that an idea which originated among people with names such as Adams, Franklin, Hamilton, Jay, Jefferson, Madison and Washington stems predominantly from Continental Europe. But the supposition that its post-war manifestation was of Continental origin may be, on the face of it, more plausible. It is therefore of particular interest that Altiero Spinelli, the greatest prophet and advocate of post-war European federalism, owed more to the British federalist writings than to any other source.

Britain is already deeply committed to the European Union and, with participation in the single currency, that commitment can only be strengthened. Thus British people need to have a better understanding of the federal idea which has been a basis for much of the Union's development, as well as of the part that the British have played in developing that idea. I hope this book will contribute to this end.

John Pinder

November 1998

ALTIERO SPINELLI AND THE BRITISH FEDERALISTS:
WRITINGS BY BEVERIDGE, ROBBINS AND SPINELLI
1937-1943

Introduction

by John Pinder

Altiero Spinelli made a remarkable contribution to the development of European Union. He was, for nearly half a century, a leader in the propagation of the idea of a federation for Europe and in political action towards that end. His final achievement, the Draft Treaty for European Union, approved by the European Parliament in 1984, gave the federal idea a constitutional form. It was also one of the impulses that led to the Single European Act, and hence to the Maastricht and Amsterdam Treaties. These have endowed the Union with the single market and the single currency; and they have given the European Parliament the power of co-decision with the Council for some half of the Union's legislation, together with the power to approve, or not, the appointment of the European Commission. These reforms go far to complete the Union's federal economic powers and a good way towards converting the Parliament and the Council into the two chambers of a federal legislature.

Political debate in Britain, by demonising the word federal, has made it difficult for British people to consider the development of the Union and its relationship with the federal idea in an objective way; and this has hampered the rational formation of Britain's European policy and the potential for constructive participation in the wider European debate. The aim of this book is to throw light on the subject by considering the basis for Spinelli's federalist thought, the little-known influence on him of British federalist writers of the late 1930s and early 1940s, and the consequences for his political action in the four decades after the end of World War Two.

How Spinelli found federalism

In 1924, when Spinelli was seventeen, he joined the young communists. Italy's democratic parties had failed to prevent Mussolini from seizing power and the Italian Communist Party had arisen as the fascists' most determined opponent. Spinelli had an urge to commit himself to an all-embracing cause and was attracted to a movement with an international vocation and a coherent theory, which offered the most active opposition to the fascists. Following the imprisonment of the Party's leaders, Spinelli himself, still less than twenty years old, assumed a leading role in what was left of its organisation. In 1927 he was arrested, then incarcerated by the fascist state for sixteen years: ten in prison, followed by six confined to prison camps.

For the first three, solitary, years he occupied himself with a kind of reading that was crucial for the development of his thought. He wanted to deepen his understanding of marxist theory. But independence of thought and criticism were fundamental to his character. He read not only marxist literature but also other writers such as Kant, Croce and Marshall, whose alternative versions of philosophy, historiography and economics profoundly impressed him.[1] When he was transferred to prisons in which discussion with other communists was possible, he tried to persuade them that, while maintaining the Party's programme of action, they should seek to improve its thinking about basic principles. This inevitably led to tensions with leaders among the other communist prisoners, who had no time for independent thought. At the same time, Spinelli became increasingly aware of Soviet tyranny, not only within the Soviet Union but also over the communist parties internationally. As he was later to write, he came to see the communist leaders as a 'politico-religious order of men who want absolute power over the rest of humanity, who don't understand and so must obey'.[2] In 1937, soon after he was transferred from prison to the less severe regime of 'confinement' in a prison camp, members of the Party were required to approve the Moscow show trials. He refused to do so and was expelled.

For two years Spinelli was a rebel without a cause. In the summer of 1939, however, in confinement on the island of Ventotene, he met Ernesto Rossi, one of the leaders of the social-liberal movement, Giustizia e Libertà. Rossi, an economics professor before his imprisonment, had been one of the favourite students of Luigi Einaudi, the liberal economist who after the war became the first President of the Italian Republic. Einaudi was a towering figure in Italian academic life, one of the few liberals who had maintained his integrity and hence his influence among a younger generation, of which Rossi was a leading member.[3] Spinelli was to write that all Rossi's 'chosen affinities' were with the eighteenth century enlightenment, especially that of Britain and France, of which he 'loved the limpid expression, the precise reasoning, the cult of rationality'. He saw in England 'the inspiration in the final instance of all the European movement towards the open market economy, towards liberty, parliamentary democracy, social reform'.[4]

Spinelli at first suspected that Rossi would, like many of an older generation of Italian liberals, be a nationalist and an economic and social conservative. But he was impressed by Rossi's 'innovative ideas' for abolishing poverty through inserting some collectivist elements in the market economy, as well as by his demonstration of the link between political despotism and public ownership of all the means of production. Before long Rossi became Spinelli's 'maestro della mente', imbuing him with the ideas of liberal constitution and market economy; and their reading of two articles by Einaudi pointed them towards the cause to which Spinelli was to devote the rest of his life: the establishment of a European federation.[5]

Already in 1918, Einaudi had, in two articles in the *Corriere della Sera*, predicted that the League of Nations, based on the national sovereignty of the member states, would not prevent another European war, and concluded that a European federation was therefore required. Rossi and Spinelli were attracted by these articles, which they read in a collection of Einaudi's essays.[6] Rossi wrote to Einaudi, asking for more to read on the subject. Einaudi, thanks to his international renown, was one of the few liberals whom the fascist regime allowed a degree of freedom that enabled him to communicate with political prisoners such as Rossi. Spinelli was to recall that Einaudi sent them some books and pamphlets written by British federalists who were active in the Federal Union movement and the Federal Union Research Institute.[7] It was not surprising that a liberal such as Einaudi was aware of British literature on the subject. Two other Piedmontese authors of similar political persuasion had published a book, also in 1918 and also advocating a European federation, and no fewer than twenty one of the twenty five sources they cited were books by authors in the British liberal tradition, including federalists such as Acton, Bryce, Seeley and Sidgwick.[8] Einaudi was also in touch with leading contemporary British economists and the books he sent included two by Lionel Robbins, which Spinelli cited several times in the two essays he wrote on Ventotene in 1942-43, and one of which he translated for the Einaudi publishing house.[9] Spinelli was unable later to remember which of the other British federalist authors he read on Ventotene and which at the League of Nations library in Geneva in 1944, but he did remember having been impressed during that period by writings of William Beveridge, Walter Layton and Barbara Wootton as well as Robbins.[10]

Spinelli did, however, recall vividly the impact of his encounter with the works of the British federalists. 'Their analysis', he wrote in the

1970s, 'of the political and economic perversion that nationalism leads to, and their reasoned presentation of the federal alternative, have remained to this day impressed on my memory like a revelation. Since I was looking for mental clarity and precision, I was not attracted by the foggy and contorted ideological federalism of a Proudhon or a Mazzini, but by the clean, precise thinking of these English federalists, in whose writings I found a very good key to understanding the chaos into which Europe was plunging and for devising alternatives'.[11]

This remarkable body of British federalist literature has not, however, remained impressed on many minds among the British themselves. The special character of Britain's experience in World War Two intervened.

Beveridge, Robbins and the British federalists

Unlike that of the Italians and most other Continental peoples, wartime experience strengthened the confidence of the British in the sovereign nation-state. After the war, Britain's political elites resisted the movement towards the sharing of sovereignty which was making such progress on the Continent, and had no difficulty in carrying the British people with them. Along with the official resistance in the 1950s to the establishment of the European Community and then to British participation in it went a rubbishing of the federal idea; and the body of literature which so much impressed Spinelli was consigned to the dustbin. The federal idea became politically taboo in both the Conservative and the Labour Party, and the word federal a target for abuse in most of the press; and during the Thatcher years the abuse reached a climax from which political debate in Britain has not yet recovered. One consequence of this prolonged neglect of rational thought about the federal principle has been an impoverishment of British policy towards the development of the European Community and Union.

The main lines of these federalists' thinking in the first half of 1940 were summarised in William Beveridge's 'Federal Tract', *Peace by Federation?*, reproduced below. The proposal was a federation of the existing European democracies plus a democratic post-war Germany. Germany had to be included in a federation designed for European security; and Beveridge argued, rightly in the event, that Germany would become democratic after the war. The other member states too had to be democratic because, as is recognised in the European Union today, a polity in which sovereignty is shared among a number of democratic states cannot allow its institutions to be prey to undemocratic forces.

The powers of the federation were to be in the fields of security and the economy, together with human rights as the guarantee of democracy; and what is now known as the principle of subsidiarity was to ensure that powers in other fields remained largely with the several member states. The federal institutions were to embody the principles of the rule of law and representative government: a federal judiciary; a federal legislature, comprising a house of the people and a house of the states; and a federal executive responsible to the legislature. Thus the proposal drew on the idea of democratic government at two levels, to deal jointly with the common problems of a group of states and separately with their internal affairs, which was invented by the American founding fathers — themselves rooted in the British political tradition. But the structure proposed for the federal government followed the British model of a parliamentary, not a presidential executive.

Beveridge was the chairman of the Federal Union Research Institute and active in Federal Union during the first months of World War Two, and hence at the centre of the brilliant group of people who were developing these ideas and applying them to the proposal for a European federation: Ivor Jennings and Kenneth Wheare, the two leading constitutional thinkers of their generation; the economists James Meade, Lionel Robbins, Barbara Wootton and Friedrich von Hayek (then a British citizen with a chair at the London School of Economics and known during that period as F.A. Hayek); and among those with a political vocation, Lord Lothian and the young Harold Wilson, who wrote a paper for the Research Institute proposing economic integration on lines foreshadowing the path that was to be followed by the European Community.[12] It was on the works of such writers that Spinelli was to base his early thinking about the concept of a European federation.

Prominent among them was Lionel Robbins, whom Beveridge, as the Director of the LSE from 1919 to 1937, had recruited to a chair of economics at the age of thirty. Robbins was an outstanding exponent of liberal economics rather than an original thinker. But he made a highly significant original contribution which has been denied due recognition, partly no doubt because of Britain's post-war anathema against the federal principle. He identified the contradiction between an international economy and the insistence on national sovereignty, which allowed international economic forces to escape a proper framework of law. 'There is', he wrote, 'world economy. But there is no world polity.'[13] The rule of law, and hence representative government to enact the laws and conduct the policies, was needed at international level, both for

5

security and to provide a legal framework for the economy. Their failure to appreciate this was, he held, a serious deficiency in nineteenth century economic liberalism; and Hayek, his colleague at the LSE, agreed. Both concluded that a federal framework was required.[14]

While Robbins's *Economic Planning and International Order*, from which an extract is given below, concentrated on the general problem of economic interdependence and the case for a federal solution, *The Economic Causes of War*, completed in the first weeks after the beginning of World War Two, concluded with a most eloquent statement, also reproduced below, of the need for a European federation, containing, as Beveridge was to propose, a democratic post-war Germany. This passage from the book that he translated for Einaudi surely had a powerful impact on Spinelli.

SPINELLI'S WRITINGS ON VENTOTENE

Federalism, as expounded in the writings of the British federalists, met Spinelli's need for a cause to which to devote his life. Spinelli and the British were an odd couple. The British breathed the air of the liberal constitution and market economy. They had only to insert the federal principle into that familiar context and apply it to European circumstances. Spinelli's political experience had been among dictatorships, first as a communist opposing Italian fascism, then as an opponent of dictatorial communism. He had no political experience of democracy; and his intensive intellectual engagement with it began when he met Rossi in the middle of 1939. What he wrote on Ventotene contained powerful critiques of both fascist and communist doctrines and practice. But he was not then versed in the workings of solid democracies or how to secure political results within them.

The first of the Ventotene documents was the Manifesto, written in mid-1941, of which Spinelli drafted all sections save one which Rossi drafted on economic and social policy within a European federation. But each of them influenced what the other wrote and they took joint responsibility for the whole. Then came Spinelli's essay on 'The United States of Europe and the Various Political Tendencies', written in the second half of 1942 and reproduced in English below; and his second essay, on marxist policy and federalist policy, which is not available in English, followed in 1943.[15] The timing has some significance, because Spinelli's encounter with federalism and his serious engagement with democracy were recent when he wrote the Manifesto, whereas by the time he wrote the essays, he had benefited from more time to digest these subjects.

Democracy

The first part of the Manifesto contained admirable statements of basic principles of liberal democracy: first, 'modern civilisation has taken the principle of freedom as its basis, a principle which holds that man must not be a mere instrument to be used by others but an autonomous centre of life'; second, 'the equal right of all citizens to participate in determining the state's will'; and third, 'the permanent value of the spirit of criticism ... against authoritarian dogmatism'. This part of the Manifesto also contained Spinelli's telling criticism of fascist states, which is more comprehensively expounded in the first pages of his essay on 'The United States of Europe and the Various Political Tendencies'.[16]

What he called 'revolutionary crises' were of much concern to Spinelli, who had reflected intensely on them during his communist period and who expected that a political vacuum, amounting to such a crisis, would follow the destruction of the fascist and nazi states. The communists, Spinelli wrote in the Manifesto, were more efficient than democracies during such crises, but lacked the ability to 'respond fully and viably to the needs of modern society'. He gave grounds for this in the section on 'Communism and European unity' in the essay on the various political tendencies and in his 'Politica marxista e politica federalista'. Both reason and the Russian experience showed that the communist economy requires bureaucratic despotism; and communism, in the attempt to remove economic inequality, leads to enormous inequality of power. The communists, like the fascists, created a 'barracks society'.[17] They could not participate in a federation. Dictatorship required a unitary state; and for the communists, the free trade that would be necessary within a federation was impossible.[18]

Understandably, in view of what he had seen of politics in Italy and neighbouring countries, Spinelli was critical of the state of the democrats and of their failure to stand up to the fascists.[19] He believed that democrats were weak in unsettled times, prone to endless polemics, a prey to the divisive tactics of interest groups and too easily brought down by events. They had also, though here he made an exception of the British, made the mistake of retaining belief in the 'mystical value' of the state.[20] Without federation, he held, such states would be drawn into an arms race and would revert to militarism. It would be impossible to put an end to the 'absolutist traditions which suffuse every pore of the modern European nation-state'.[21] German democracy in particular would not be possible save in a European federation. So federation would have to be established soon after the war was won. Otherwise, democracy would not survive and there would again be war.

Spinelli later criticised what he had written in the Manifesto because, among other things, he had failed to foresee that post-war Europe would be heavily conditioned by outside influences.[22] The presence of American forces in Western Europe and Soviet forces in Eastern Europe did indeed ensure that there would be no wars between states within those areas. The prevention of war became a matter of relations between the United States and the Soviet Union, not, as Spinelli and the British federalists too had expected, between Germany and its European neighbours.

Within Western Europe, the physical constraint of the American presence made war impossible. It also gave time for the European Community to be created and to develop, thus providing a context within which war could be superseded by law and politics as a means of dealing with problems in the relations between the member states. This process of moving by stages towards a federal system, through adding competences and reforming institutions of a community that had been endowed at the outset with some federal elements, had not been foreseen by Spinelli, nor by the British writers who had contributed so much to his initial federalist impulse. But acquiring its own political momentum, this process of federalisation by stages provided the context within which war between the member states became seen as out of the question.

Another way in which the American presence gainsaid Spinelli's prediction about post-war Europe was the establishment in Germany of a stable liberal democracy without the context of a European federation, though within the developing European Community. In the western part of Germany the Americans, with an important contribution by the British, helped German democrats to found the Federal Republic, with its model democratic constitution and with political forces capable of ensuring the consolidation of a successful democratic polity. Without giving much thought to the way in which it would be achieved, the British federalists had been more optimistic than Spinelli about the future for democracy in Germany. Confident that it was the better and stronger system, and that Germans, following defeat in war, would realise this to be so, these British expected the victors to be dealing with a democratic post-war Germany. But Spinelli was more conscious of the weaknesses of democrats than of their strengths: understandably at that time and place, when he had been closer to the failures of the democrats in Italy,

Germany and some neighbouring countries than to their strength beyond. The Manifesto, in assuming that democratic states could not survive in a post-war Europe unless a federation was rapidly established, may therefore fail to bring home to Europeans today the fundamental challenge for democracy: that the great political problems which stem from the interdependence among states with respect to security, economy and environment escape the reach of the democratic process, unless that process is applied to the common affairs of groups of interdependent states as well as within the states themselves. Democracy is emptied of essential parts of its content unless it is established at a federal level too.

Federation

Germany, which posed the problem of the absolutely sovereign nation-state in its most acute form, could not, in the words of the Manifesto, be 'broken in pieces or held on a chain once it is conquered'. The solution to this, as to other crucial problems, was to abolish 'the division of Europe into national, sovereign states' and to establish a 'steady federal state'.[23] The Manifesto outlined only briefly the powers that the federation would require: to control a European army, to break with economic autarky, and to have sufficient means to accomplish these things. The federated states would at the same time retain their autonomy with respect to their own political life.

The essay on 'The United States of Europe and the Various Political Tendencies' was more precise.[24] The powers would include the control of foreign policy as well as of armed forces. All protectionist barriers would be abolished and there would be a single currency. Free movement of people across the internal frontiers would be ensured. Ethnic minorities would be protected. Along with Beveridge, Spinelli also proposed federal responsibilities for the administration of colonies, which then covered much of the southern part of the world. For exercising all these powers, Spinelli proposed a federal judiciary, an administration independent of those of the member states, the right to raise the necessary taxes, and a federal legislature based on the direct participation of the citizens and not on representation of the member states: similar to the institutional system proposed by the British federalists, save that Spinelli did not mention that the administration would be responsible to the legislature, nor did he specify that there would be two chambers, in one of which senators would be elected from each member state.

This federation would be, Spinelli wrote, 'the grandest creation' in Europe for centuries. It would lead to peaceful co-operation with American and Asian peoples, 'waiting for a more distant future when the unity of the entire world will become possible'. It would, as British federalists, who likewise envisaged eventual world unity, also believed, be the biggest step towards world peace.[25]

For Spinelli, the political idea was the prelude to political action. His critique of the problem of sovereignty and outline of the federal solution drew heavily on those of the British federalists. But his analysis of the forces for and against the federation, as a basis for effective action, was his own.

First, in order to be sure that a European federation was a sustainable project, he analysed the forces that would support it once it had been established. The 'highest and most fertile element' among the intellectuals, steeped in Europe's common cultural roots, would be favourable.[26] So would the workers, who would benefit from improved economic conditions in the federation and who should be ideologically sympathetic; and democratic trade unions have indeed been supportive of federal steps in the Community and, in many cases, of the federal idea. Spinelli, doubtless influenced by Rossi and the writings of liberals such as Robbins, also added the more dynamic entrepreneurs to his list. While still stressing the role of the working class, he was moving away from the class analysis with which he had as a communist lived for so long. In the Manifesto, he had already shifted the line between progressives and reactionaries away from that between more, or less, socialism and redrawn it between those who focused on gaining national political power and those whose main aim would be 'the creation of a solid international state'.[27] In his 'Politica marxista e politica federalista', written nearly two years later, he stressed that the divisions which counted were not those between classes, but those between liberal and protectionist bourgeoisie, and between the workers who struggle for general emancipation and those who pursue an egoistic sectional or class policy.[28] Federation would be a public good, with a dynamic economy and lower military expenditure, which the citizens should be able to appreciate, while the forces that benefit from protectionism and from their positions of power within the nation-states would progressively decline.

The Manifesto also affirmed, in a section drafted by Rossi, that federation would enable 'the struggle against social inequalities and privileges to be restored'.[29] The goal was to be the emancipation of the working classes and the creation of more humane conditions for them. The constitutional context was to be representative government and the rule of law based on fundamental freedoms, including freedom of the press, the right of assembly, the right to join a trade union of one's choice and 'the possibility for all citizens to participate effectively in the state's life'. There was to be education and training for all. A decent living standard was to be guaranteed, 'regardless of whether a person is able to work or not'. Land was to be redistributed to the peasants and in industry there would be co-operatives and employee profit-sharing. Private property would be limited or extended according to the circumstances, not to any dogmatic principle, though there would be large-scale nationalisation of enterprises such as national monopolies. The Manifesto did not propose that policy in such fields would be a federal responsibility. Their relevance to the federal project was, rather, that they would 'create very broad-based support around the new institutional system from a large number of citizens', through a political orientation such as became normal in post-war Europe among the parties of the centre and centre-left.

While Spinelli was confident that a federation was sustainable, he thought there would be no chance of establishing it in stable conditions, when the existing structures of states would be stronger than the forces working for change. He was, however, convinced that the war would be followed by a great political crisis, with the states of Continental Europe broken and no powerful state structures to stand in the way. Another of his subsequent criticisms of the Manifesto was its assumption that the federation would be rapidly established;[30] and as a consequence it ignored the longer haul during which the federalists would have to contend with established state structures. He and Rossi did realise that Britain would end the war with such a structure intact, but nevertheless hoped, for a while, that a post-war Labour government might lead Europe to federation — only to be disillusioned in the event.[31] In the political vacuum on the Continent, the Manifesto argued, people would want real peace but not know how to secure it. Federalists had the answer and the way would be open for their campaign.

Spinelli appreciated the role of men of ideas, 'advisers' as he called them in his second essay: thinkers (who may no longer be alive) giving ideas to political men of action 'whose principal passion consists in the work of organisation and of the command of men'.[32] There had been federalist thinkers, but not the necessary men of action. The need now was for effective political leaders and activists, working for feasible objectives. Many people would benefit from the federalist project, freeing the European market to create a single, healthy European economy and cutting defence spending, thus releasing resources for welfare. But only a dedicated minority would act. So the principal problem was the formation of a federalist movement to take advantage of the favourable conditions that would follow the end of the war.[33]

After Ventotene: from ideas to action

The foundation of a federalist movement that would lead to the establishment of a post-war European federation was already central to Spinelli's thinking when he drafted the Ventotene Manifesto. The Manifesto concluded with a ringing declaration of the need for such a movement, in terms which Spinelli later criticised as 'ephemeral ... because too crudely Leninist'.[34] That concluding section began with the words 'the revolutionary party', which was to recruit, from the 'gradually increasing circle of sympathisers', members 'who have identified and accepted the European revolution as the main goal in their lives, who carry out the necessary work with strict discipline ... even in the most dangerously illegal situations'.[35] The illegal situations were, of course, those that would confront the members of a such a movement within a fascist state, such as Italy at that time; and the concept of the movement outlined in the Manifesto was no doubt 'too crudely Leninist' because Spinelli's political experience had largely been within the communist party. The aim of the movement that he envisaged was, however, not an autocracy nor a bureaucracy, but 'resolutely to create from the outset the conditions for individual freedom'; and after his liberation from confinement, Spinelli rapidly learnt to apply the practices of democratic politics.

Along with the political line of division that he drew between those whose main aim was to gain national power and those who would strive to create an international state, Spinelli felt that the other significant new contribution of the Manifesto was to regard federation, not just as a beautiful ideal, but as an objective that required political action now. He did not then know of the achievements of Britain's Federal Union movement in the period 1938-40, which organised a campaign that was said to have made 'a staggeringly effective appeal to the British mind', and which won the editorial support of *The Guardian*, *The Times* and the *New Statesman*.[36] Thus public support was delivered for a federalist policy on the part of the British government but, after France fell, the project of a union with Britain, France and Germany found little resonance in Britain. R.W.G. Mackay, as a Labour MP in the post-war House of Commons, nevertheless in 1948 secured some two hundred signatures, in approximately equal numbers from both Labour and Conservative MPs, for a resolution that called for a long-term policy to create a European federation, to be designed by a constituent assembly which the governments in Western Europe should convoke as soon as possible. Prime Minister Attlee, while rejecting any idea of absolute sovereignty, courteously rebuffed the resolution.[37] Mackay certainly saw federation as an objective that required 'political action now'; and he continued his parliamentary activity until it became clear that British politics had become set in an anti-federalist mould. Mackay died in 1960, leaving behind him the text for a book entitled *Towards the United States of Europe*.[38] Meanwhile, Spinelli too had become a practitioner of the arts of democratic politics that were second nature to Mackay.

Directly after his liberation from Ventotene in 1943, Spinelli initiated the foundation of the Movimento Federalista Europeo and then took steps towards the formation of the federalist movement at European level. In the early 1950s, when the project for a European Defence Community was making headway, Spinelli played a major part in persuading Prime Minister De Gasperi that a European Army would have to be responsible to a democratic European government within the framework of a federal constitution.[39] A paper he wrote to this effect attracted Jean Monnet, who invited him in 1952 to draft the addresses which Monnet, as the first President of the High Authority, was to present to its inaugural meeting and to that of the parliamentary Assembly of the European Coal and Steel Community. These addresses expounded the federal elements in the new Community.[40] Monnet then invited Spinelli to stay and draft for him a series of texts that would comprise a comprehensive statement along the lines of *The Federalist* of Hamilton, Jay and Madison. But Spinelli's response was that he preferred to enter the European institutions later as a politician rather than immediately as an official.[41] The Italian government, influenced by Spinelli, had meanwhile proposed, and Italy's partners in the Community agreed, that the constitutional document be drafted by the Assembly of the ECSC (which was slightly enlarged for the purpose), in the form of a treaty establishing a European Political Community alongside the treaty for the European Defence Community. Spinelli worked closely with Paul-Henri Spaak, who was President of the Assembly, to ensure that a viable treaty was drafted and approved by the Assembly. While the EDC treaty was signed by all six Community member states and ratified by Germany and the Benelux countries, it ran into political difficulties in France and was shelved by the Assemblée Nationale in August 1954; and the project for a Political Community fell with it. But this first half of the 1950s had shown how effective Spinelli had already become in federalist action in the democratic and parliamentary context.

The failure of the project for the EDC and the EPC was a bitter blow. Monnet's reaction, to build further on the existing Community, led to the Messina conference and the establishment of the European Economic Community. But Spinelli failed to appreciate the potential of this approach and abandoned the method of working through parliaments and governments in favour of a campaign to arouse the citizens to elect representatives to a Congress of the European People, which he intended should itself draft a federal constitution. The campaign failed and Spinelli steered clear of politics through most of the 1960s.

By 1970, however, Spinelli had accepted that the Community offered a basis for federalist political action and secured appointment as one of the two Italian members of the Commission, thus gaining experience of the Community's political system. Then in 1976, already aged nearly seventy, his parliamentary career began, with his election to the Italian Chamber of Deputies as an independent supported by the Italian Communist Party. When asked whether he had returned to his earlier communist commitment, his answer was threefold: that the Italian communists had, on the contrary, moved far towards his position, with respect to both Europe and parliamentary democracy; that as an independent, he would in no way be bound by the communists' policy but would pursue his own line; and that since it was the communists who were willing to put him on their list of parliamentary candidates, this was the only way in which he could pursue that line through parliamentary action.[42]

Spinelli, the European Parliament and the Draft Treaty

Spinelli soon won a place in the Italian delegation to the European Parliament, still indirectly elected through the parliaments of member states. He thus acquired knowledge of the workings of the Parliament before being elected an MEP when its democratic legitimacy was enhanced through the first direct elections in 1979. The governments had, finally, taken the decision to provide the representatives directly elected by European citizens, which he had failed to secure by voluntary action in the late 1950s.

Spinelli lost no time in seeking to persuade the Parliament that it should draft a European constitution which could lift the Community out of its current malaise. Through the following five years he showed not only intense commitment but also outstanding talent as a parliamentarian in that task of persuasion: securing the establishment of the Committee on Institutional Affairs and becoming its general rapporteur; creating within it a group of MEPs who shared the commitment to drafting a federalist Treaty of European Union; and ensuring enough support among the Parliament's major political groups to secure a majority of 237 votes to 31 to approve the Draft Treaty in February 1984. He worked particularly well with British MEPs. Of the eight MEPs who responded to his initial proposal that the Parliament set the process of treaty revision in train, and who were present at the dinner at the Crocodile Restaurant when the Crocodile group which promoted the project from start to finish was founded, three were British.[43] Members of the then Conservative majority among the British MEPs played a major part in the Institutions Committee, one of whom emphasised Spinelli's ability to 'compromise and synthesise' in order to reach agreement among the different political groups.[44]

The wheel had come full circle. The drafter of the Ventotene Manifesto, who had envisaged a federalist movement in 'too crudely Leninist' terms, had devoted himself to the parliamentary method and become a consummate parliamentarian. The man who had scorned the Monnet method of building federal Europe by stages had worked to reform the Community through the Draft Treaty, which designed a federal reform of the institutions, to be endowed with the necessary federal economic powers, but not with the power over armed force that would make it a federal state. The Draft Treaty offered the potential for the transfer of such power to the Union. But Spinelli, in order to secure its approval, accepted that the Treaty would fall short of providing for a federal state. While that remained his aim, it would have to remain subject to further decision when political constraints allow.

The Draft Treaty being approved by the Parliament during the French Presidency of the Council, Spinelli seized the opportunity to visit President Mitterrand and secured his support for the project. Mitterrand initiated a high-level committee to put to the European Council proposals on institutional affairs; and the committee, containing several supporters of the Parliament's project, recommended a new treaty establishing European Union, to be based on the existing Communities and 'guided by the spirit and method of the Draft Treaty voted by the European Parliament'.[45] The report was on the European Council's agenda when it met in June 1985 and decided to convene the Intergovernmental Conference that drafted the Single European Act, which enhanced the role of the Parliament as well as providing for the single market and more majority voting in the Council. Spinelli criticised the Single Act, on which the governments reached agreement shortly before he died in 1986, as a 'dead mouse'. But in the following years it became, rather, a mouse that roared, relaunching the Community on a path which led not only to the single currency, but also to a further strengthening of the Parliament's powers that has brought it half way towards becoming the legislative equal of the Council.

Thus Spinelli played his part in the process of building the Union by stages, which had been initiated by Monnet and had, since the 1950s, been supported by British federalists who saw it as a politically feasible route towards the federation which their pre-war predecessors had envisaged. But the political climate in Britain, undefeated in the war and with undiminished belief in the viability of the nation-state, limited their opportunity to become a mainstream influence on British policy. In Italy, to the contrary, confidence in the nation-state had been shattered by fascism and its consequences. The message of the Ventotene Manifesto, written from the perspective of a people emerging from the fascist experience, had a powerful impact on Italian opinion. Spinelli, rapidly learning the rules of the game of democratic politics, became a political force both in Italy and at the European level. Italy remains the most federalist European country and the movement that Spinelli founded retains its capacity to sustain Italian commitment to the objective of a federal European constitution. The European Union itself, with the single market, single currency, rule of law ensured by the Court of Justice, majority voting in the Council for the bulk of European legislation and power of the Parliament over some half of it, has, through the incremental process envisaged by Monnet, put in place substantial elements of the constitution that was the goal of Spinelli and of the British federalists who inspired him. It is to be hoped that this book on the British and Italian origins of post-war federalist thinking, and on some examples of the way in which federal principles have been applied in the development of the European Community and Union, will contribute to a better understanding of these principles and of ways in which they can inform the Union's future development.

Beveridge's Proposal for a Federal Europe

Introductory Note

Sir William Beveridge (1879-1963, later Lord Beveridge), after working as a social researcher, became a civil servant. Winston Churchill, then President of the Board of Trade, chose him as personal assistant and by 1918 he had become, as Permanent Secretary of the Ministry of Food, one of the youngest heads of a department in the history of the British Civil Service. From 1919 to 1937 he was the Director of the London School of Economics, which he transformed from a small college with mainly part-time students to a world leader in the social sciences. Among the staff whom he attracted to the LSE were four outstanding scholars who made important contributions to the contemporary federalist literature: Ivor Jennings, Harold Laski, Lionel Robbins and Friedrich von Hayek. In 1937 he became Master of University College, Oxford, and in 1939-40 he was active in the Federal Union movement and Chairman of the Federal Union Research Institute. He was then asked by the British government to make proposals for policy on social security after the war and the Beveridge report on 'Social Security and Allied Services', presented to Parliament in 1942, became the foundation stone of the welfare state. After the war he was for a time the President of Federal Union and a Trustee of the Federal Trust, but was by then interested in the idea of world rather than European federation.

As Chairman of the Federal Union Research Institute from September 1939, he again attracted the best available people to take part in its studies of the constitutional and economic aspects of a federation to include Britain, France, Belgium, the Netherlands and the Scandinavian states, to be founded after the war together with a Germany that had returned to democracy. Beveridge chaired the Institute's constitutional and economic committees, which included, as well as Hayek, Jennings and Robbins from the LSE, other stars such as James Meade, Kenneth Wheare and Barbara Wootton, together with a future Prime Minister, Harold Wilson. Beveridge's *Peace by Federation?*, the first of a series of Federal Tracts, was published on 1 May 1940 by Federal Union and again in September 1940 by the Royal Institute of International Affairs in a series of World Order Papers. The remaining Federal Tracts were published by the Federal Union Research Institute. Beveridge's Tract brought together the thinking of the remarkable people then active around Federal Union and the Institute, to present a coherent proposal for the institutions, powers and membership of a European federation. The main purpose of the federation would be to secure permanent peace among the member states. The text is reproduced intact below, except for two passages containing contemporary detail about European politics that is no longer relevant to the argument, a section on the treatment of member states' colonies which is now also redundant, and a table showing areas and populations of proposed member states. The question mark in the title did not, Beveridge explained towards the end of the Tract, imply doubt that the federation he proposed would, if established by the wishes of the peoples concerned, bring them lasting peace, but rather whether it would in fact be established. Half a century after the end of World War Two, Beveridge's question is still waiting for an answer.

J.P.

Peace by Federation?

by Sir William Beveridge

In a world already darkened by wars, the problem of world order can be approached in two ways — general and special. Generally, we may examine the causes of war, the possible types of relation between nations, and the means for securing that disputes between them are settled by pacific means. Specially, we may consider the origins and circumstances of a particular war now in progress, the probable conditions of its ending, and the terms of settlement which are most likely both to prevent a repetition of that war and to lay foundations of permanent and general peace. No excuse is needed for choosing in this paper the second line of approach, through consideration of the war in which Britain and her allies are now engaged against Germany. This approach means examining the problem of world order in the first instance from the point of view of a particular group of nations — Britain and her allies — but that is the natural point of view for a British writer. It need not involve inability at a later stage to correct the national equation of the writer by reference to wider interests. It has the advantage of practicality. The foundations of world order must be laid on facts, on the geography, economics, and psychology of particular nations, rather than on reasoning about nations in general.

Choice of this line of approach involves a particular point of view, to be widened later. It involves also two assumptions which should be stated. One assumption is that, in ending this war, Britain and her allies will find themselves in a position to secure, either by dictation or by agreement, peace terms of the kind that they desire; if this cannot be assumed, the writing of pamphlets on world order is irrational. Another assumption is that Britain and her allies desire and will continue to desire in making peace, not to end this war only, but to stamp out the seeds of future war.

The actual approach to peace, as it unfolds itself from the events of war in the months or years that lie ahead, may look very different from these assumptions. To contemplate defeat for the allied nations in their own borders is unprofitable as well as unjustified pessimism. But if the war is prolonged there will come hints of peace and offers of mediation, reflecting the shifting balance of military events. There may come chances of securing by agreement without victory what looks like nearly all the allies want but may be something far short of it. There may come periods of frustration, when, as in 1916, the allied leaders find themselves weighing possible gains by continuing the war against the certain relief of stopping it, and will be setting hope of release from bloodshed for unknown future generations against the lives of the generation that they know. In 1916 the decision to continue was sustained by hope of a final settlement with war itself. In November 1918 these hopes seemed to be realised. In the mood of 1919, when nearly all the great nations of the world were exhausted by war or hating it with passion, it seemed possible, and it was taken as a practical aim, to banish war for ever from the earth. The basic assumption of this paper is the aim, if not the mood, of 1919.

THE BRITISH COMMONWEALTH, FRANCE AND GERMANY

'It is ... comparatively easy to patch up a peace which will last for thirty years; what is difficult ... is to draw up a peace which will not provoke a fresh struggle when those who have had practical experience of what war means have passed away.'[46] So wrote Mr Lloyd George on March 25, 1919, in a memorandum designed to resist the desire of the French for a military frontier on the Rhine and in place thereof to base on justice a peace that should be permanent.

The memorandum achieved its immediate object. The plan of Marshal Foch for establishing the Rhine as a barrier against German attack was rejected. The Treaty of Versailles was signed on June 8, 1919. The peace thus established has lasted just twenty years, not thirty years, not an eternity. What are the reasons for this tragic defeat of expectations? What lessons should be drawn from it for guidance in the future?

One view is that in 1919 Marshal Foch was right and Mr Lloyd George was wrong — that the Treaty of Versailles erred, not by excessive severity of the terms imposed upon the beaten enemy, but through their weakness. If we ask, however, whether a military frontier on the Rhine would have guaranteed the peace of Europe, the question, in 1940, is answered in the negative as soon as it is asked. A barrier on the Rhine would have been irrelevant to the defence of Czecho-Slovakia or Poland

— or Britain or Roumania. A barrier on the Rhine is no barrier to aircraft; one cannot build a Maginot Line 20,000 feet high in the air.

Another and commoner view is that the Treaty of Versailles failed through its injustice and vindictiveness. That Treaty contains some features, such as reparations and the war guilt clause which few people would defend today. It contains provisions as to colonies which nothing but casuistry can seek to reconcile with the Armistice terms. But it does not deserve one-tenth of the facile abuse that has been heaped upon it. The worst inequities of the last war settlement, such as the failure to implement minority provisions, and the Italo-Austrian border, are no part of the Treaty of Versailles. The boundaries drawn elsewhere than on the Brenner Pass might easily have been much the same, if they had been the subject of adjudication by an impartial tribunal after hearing all parties, in place of being dictated by allied and associated powers. More than this, the Treaty of Versailles contained a genuine attempt to establish a new world order and to enthrone justice in place of war as the arbiter amongst nations.

The plan of 1919 for this purpose failed completely, less through lack of will than through lack of knowledge, through failure to understand the new conditions of peace in Europe and the changes of old habits and institutions that were required to secure it. If to the passionate desire for peace that filled the world in 1919 we could add the experience of the past twenty years, what should be now proposed? What are the real lessons of those years?

The first lesson, which it would be foolish to ignore and dishonest to conceal with false-friendly phrases, is that there can be no assurance of peace with justice in Europe so long as the German people can have arms at their discretion. This is not the whole truth about national armaments, but it is true and lies at the root of the European problem. The powers of organisation and discipline of this highly talented and numerous people in a central situation in Europe, combined with their readiness to hand over their destinies, time and again, to leaders whose creed is power, leave no other conclusion possible than that the condition of permanent peace in Europe is permanent disarmament of Germany.

How and on what terms can the permanent disarmament of Germany be secured?

One plan has been tried already in 1919 — enforced unilateral disarmament of Germany coupled with promises by other nations (under the fourth of the Fourteen Points) to reduce their arms 'to the lowest point consistent with domestic safety'. Under this plan most nations other than Germany remained heavily armed, yet the nations most concerned — Britain and France — failed to stop re-armament of Germany. Between 1934 and 1938 the world received an impressive demonstration of the unwillingness of the British and French democracies to fight on an uneasy conscience or to look ahead. It may be said that such lethargy would not be repeated. If Germany could once again be disarmed by victorious democracies, even the democracies could be trusted to keep her disarmed for ever. The Foch prescription of military occupation of the Rhine would be converted into military domination.

Already voices are being raised, in this country and in France, urging that their peace aim should be to break up Germany once more. ... But we cannot put the clock back seventy years by force and keep it back except by continuing force.

I do not believe that a peace plan of this nature would commend itself to public opinion in Britain at any time, or to enduring public opinion in France; it would be rejected by the rest of the world. In any case it is impracticable and out of date. In 1919 it was possible to think of German disarmament as a prelude to general disarmament; there had been a world war making a world weary of war. The conflict today is limited and may remain limited. However it ends, however weary of war the principal belligerents may be, there will be other nations in Europe, not exhausted by war, not ready to disarm. Above all, there will be Russia. All plans for merely reducing Germany to impotence, by disarmament or by forcible disunion, ignore one of the main elements in the situation — the Russian Revolution. They involve a permanent military occupation of all Germany in force sufficient both to keep Germany down and to keep Russia out, Russia and the Comintern.

To say this is not to take sides in the dispute between socialism and capitalism, planned or other, as methods for organising the economic activities of mankind. Socialism is consistent with preservation of essential liberties and is consistent with peace and justice between nations. If socialism were ever established in Britain by the will of the people it would not make the citizen less free in essentials or threaten other nations with war. But Soviet Communism today is another thing altogether — a tyranny which to many socialists makes socialism seem not worth the Russian price, a tyranny become as shameless in aggression as is Hitlerism itself. Today the one redeeming virtue of Soviet Communism in the eyes of other nations is its probable inefficiency in organising war. This virtue would not be found in Communism of like spirit established in Germany. By the sacrifice of millions of lives from 1914 to 1918 the

Allied and Associated Powers exorcised hereditary militant autocracy from Germany, and made a home for Hitlerism. If now Britain and France are able to exorcise Hitlerism, but do no more, they will leave a land swept clear of hope and garnished with hate, a fit dwelling for a worse spirit still.

The French feel, with justice, that in 1919 they were cheated of security. They will want on this occasion, if they can, as the British will want, to be done with danger from Germany once and for all. They will not think that they are done with danger, merely through a change of government in Germany. 'Hitler made the war, but the Germans made Hitler.' 'Germany left to herself will always produce Hitlers.' Those are typical summings up of the situation in the French press and it is difficult to deny their justice. The French people, in M. Daladier's words, will not on this occasion lay down their arms without 'material guarantees' against German aggression in the future. They ought not to be asked to do so, by the British or by anyone else.

But 'material guarantees' are not to be found in merely reducing Germany to impotence. They have to be sought, rather, along another line, also indicated by a distinguished leader of French opinion, M. Léon Blum. The material guarantees for the security and peace of other nations in Europe are to be sought through 'the integration of Germany into a European system'. What M. Blum had in mind in this phrase is shown by another passage written by him a few days before: 'The independence and security of peoples in a federated and disarmed Europe must be guaranteed.'[47] More recently the French Prime Minister, M. Daladier, has said: 'It will be necessary ... perhaps to envisage federal ties between the various states of Europe.' [48]

These leaders of French opinion point the way in which the world should move. ...

Granted that dictatorships are more likely than democracies to lead to war, what leads to dictatorships? Historically, the Nazi dictatorship is the channel through which the German people have expressed their sense of economic suffering and national injustice. Germany must ultimately be made peaceful in accord with her own desires and not against them. She must be allowed to share the economic opportunities which in her view make peace easy for the democracies.

'Left to herself, Germany will always produce Hitlers.' She cannot be left to herself. Germany cannot be allowed to have arms of her own, if Europe is to have security, but she cannot be left unarmed. There must be arms to protect Germany; ultimately, if not forthwith, they must be arms shared by her with others. She must be integrated into a European system — on the terms not of servitude but of partnership. When Germany is ready to return to civilisation, she must be embraced, not as an enemy, but as a friend.

Europe in many American eyes is a prize-ring. After each round the victor of that round has gone about his business; the loser left in his corner has nursed himself back to strength and vengeance in the next round. Wars so ended settle nothing. But in earlier stages of human history wars might settle things; they might end in conquest which is one way to lasting peace. The third course, the way of the future, superseding both conquest and the prize-ring, is partnership. If the present war is to end by laying the foundations of international order in Europe, it must end by a union in which Britain, France and Germany shall at last make war between them impossible for ever. Peace must come by their federation.

A PEACE FEDERATION

Federalism is not new in the world or in the experience of Britons: the United States of America, Switzerland, Canada, Australia, are federations of proved success. The new departure now proposed in world government is federation across long established national boundaries.

On any such proposal three questions arise at the outset. What nation-states should be included in the federation? What should be the division of powers between the federal and the national governments? What should be the form of the federal government? Needless to say, these questions cannot be answered fully here. Nor are the answers given put forward dogmatically; they are intended only to illustrate the nature and purpose of the main proposal. ...

States for inclusion

First, as to the states to be included. The proposal for federation in this paper is a peace proposal, designed in ending the present war to establish a barrier against future wars. It is a 'Peace Federation' and the states envisaged as its members are all those who as belligerents or as neutrals have been most deeply concerned in the present war and will have suffered by it. This means in Europe, Britain, France and Germany as belligerents, Denmark, Norway, Sweden, Finland, Belgium, Holland, Switzerland, and Eire as neutrals;* it means, outside Europe, the four

---

* *Editor's note.* Italy was not yet a belligerent.

self-governing Dominions of the British Commonwealth who are belligerent — Australia, Canada, New Zealand, and South Africa. The treatment of Poland and Czecho-Slovakia, when they are restored, depends upon other possible groupings in Europe.

The following comments explain the choice of countries for federation:

(a) The area is limited and therefore manageable. The federal principle is not now, if it ever will be, applicable to world government. The states suggested have a population of 235,000,000 in a total area of 8,822,000 square miles. This is a little more than the U.S.S.R. in area and about a third greater in population. It is rather more than twice the area of the U.S.A. and rather less than twice the population. With the exception of the British Dominions (considered specially below) the states are contiguous to one another.

(b) The states have to a large extent a common culture, comparable standards of life, close economic relations, and all but one of them is already democratic. The exception — Germany — has been democratic from 1919 to 1933 and before 1914 had a strong and growing democratic movement. As is explained below, practical considerations of government make it necessary to limit federation to effective democracies, i.e. to exclude dictatorships and one-party states.

(c) The inclusion of Germany is essential to making the federation an organ of assured peace. If she is in, the neighbouring neutrals will have every reason for coming in, for certain security. Without Germany, the federation will look too much like an alliance against fascist states. The adhesion of the neutrals is important for two reasons. First, they will hold the balance of power in the federal government, between those who are now belligerent. Second, as small nations they take naturally the right view of human values; they pursue the happiness of the common people because they cannot provide glory for rulers.

(d) The inclusion of the four British Dominions and Eire, while not essential, is highly desirable. Clearly Britain could not go into a European federation turning her back upon the British Commonwealth. She could not enter herself except after full consultation with the self-governing Dominions and regard for their views; if they were not willing to join but Britain did join, she would have to preserve a special relation to them. But their experience in the working of democratic and federal institutions would be invaluable; two of them — Canada and South Africa — already combine populations of different European origins; some at least would continue to need the security against other powers that federal membership would secure. The geographical position of the Dominions, outside Europe, might be a reason for admitting them on special terms, e.g. with a recognised right of secession not accorded to others. But their position outside Europe is another reason for bringing them into the suggested federation if possible. The federation is a federation in the world, not outside the world; a step towards world order and co-operation, not a move towards isolation.

(e) The relation of India to the federation raises a special problem. Negatively it is clear that India could not be brought into the federation as an additional state on the same terms as the rest without changing its character. India is of Asia, not of Europe or of Europe exported to other continents; she is large enough and populous enough to require federation on her own account. The logical immediate answer on the problem of India is to say that the federation would stand to India in whatever relation Britain stood at the time when Britain joined the federation; whatever responsibilities for external defence or internal order of India remained to Britain then would be undertaken by the federation. But it would be equally possible for Britain within the federation to maintain special relations with India and the means of giving effect to them.

Division of powers

In regard to the division of powers between federal and national government, this should follow the American plan of giving named powers to the federal government and leaving to the national governments everything that is neither transferred to the federal government, nor reserved to the people by constitutional guarantees. The problem is thus one of defining what powers shall be transferred to the federal government as dealing with 'common affairs'. The answer is best given in three stages.

Defence and Foreign Policy. Two affairs are certainly common and form the minimum for transfer, viz. defence and foreign policy. This means, in the end, that all the armed forces of all the federated nations will become a single force, owing allegiance to the federal government and not to the national governments. There will be no *British* Navy, no *German* Army, no *French* Air Force, but British, German, French, Swedish, Belgian and other contingents of a federal navy, army and air force.

To many this will be a hard saying — at first, perhaps, too hard to be accepted. Those who find pooling of all arms in a federation unthinkable must face the alternatives. Is it worth while to keep a British Navy at cost of there being a German Army and a German Air Force? Is it feasible to keep British and French armaments while denying them to others? That was tried in 1919, with results known to all. If Britain and her allies were once again in the dominant position of 1919, there would be temptation to ensure security for themselves by their own arms. Could they trust themselves, would they be trusted by others, not to abuse power, not to use it for economic gain? An alternative of another type is that one form of armed force — say that of the air — should be made international or super-national, while other forms remain under national control. It is difficult to see merit in such a compromise. If the force which remains national is of such a scale that it can challenge the super-national force, it may become the basis of aggressive civil war. If not, it is a delusive safeguard; it makes armed conflict and bloodshed possible for no advantage.

The steps by which the pooling of the armed forces of an international federation could be brought about depend on the circumstances in which the federation came to birth. The military aspects of accomplished federation need expert consideration. But if the peoples wish to get security through federation, it is hard to suppose that the military problem of guaranteeing their security against civil war would prove insoluble. Critics of federation often cite the American Civil War as proof that federation may fail to prevent war between member states. The reply to this criticism is that the American Civil War occurred 75 years ago, and that since that time there have been two revolutions — one in arms and one in the minds of men. First, in the America of 1860 the simple arms required were available to all; every man had his musket. The aeroplanes, tanks, submarines and scientific equipment of modern warfare are not broadcast and cannot be improvised. So simple a device as making guns in one part of the federation and the shells to fit them in another part might prove an effective safeguard against revolution or forcible secession. Second, war in the minds of all peoples who know it bears an aspect today very different from its aspect even a generation ago: to talk of civilised man as a fighting animal, when fighting means modern totalitarian war, is patently ridiculous. War threatens to die of inanition in the minds of thoughtful men. The greatest danger to civilisation today is not the risk that war will go on for ever, but that the more civilised nations will abandon war too soon, before others do, and will leave the world to the oppressors.

The ordinary citizen today does not have to be kept from fighting; the ordinary citizen to-morrow, fresh from new experience of war, will be ready to barter arms for security. The men of the fighting professions will not find anything unthinkable in federation. The traditions and spirit of those who in different nations choose the risks of the fighting professions have much in common. The British Navy becoming, as at first it naturally would be, the main part of a federal navy, would find no difficulty in keeping the peace of the seas with a wider loyalty.

Dependencies. ... *

Currency, Trade, Migration. There remains as the third stage of discussion, the problem of economic affairs. Should any of these be regarded as common and transferred to the federal authority, or should they all be left to the national authorities? This raises technical questions of great complexity on which no final answer can be given.

Mr Clarence Streit, in his projected federation of fifteen democracies including the United States, contemplates within this area a single currency and absolute freedom of trade and migration. It may be doubted whether all the practical consequences of this proposal have been envisaged by him, in relation to the financial and economic systems of the countries concerned and their differing standards of wages. It is probably wiser to assume that even if currency, trade and migration were treated as common affairs, so that the federal authority had power to deal with them, the authority would decide that some barriers and differences between the separate states should continue at least for a period.

---

* *Editor's Note.* Beveridge proposed that the aim of the administration of colonies should be to prepare the inhabitants to become 'full citizens of the modern world', and that, until this preparation issued in self-government, their interests should be paramount. He suggested that meanwhile the federal government should have 'powers of supervision and control'. The detail of this section is omitted as no longer relevant.

The question of how much economic power should be given to the federal authority is essentially a question of how far the different nations are prepared to go towards unity. Very considerable transfer of economic powers from the national to the federal authority — extending to final control over currency, trade and migration — is probably the ideal. Economic activities are already to a large extent international. Economic problems, such as cyclical fluctuation of trade, are common and call for international or super-national solutions. Foreign policy in the modern world is largely concerned with economics; it is difficult to envisage a federal authority unable to negotiate commercial treaties with states outside the federation, but every such negotiation involves the economic interests of one or more member-states. The federal authority will have a stronger hold on the loyalty of all its citizens and will grow in the unity which makes strength, if it has common constructive tasks of peace, not merely armaments and foreign policy within its sphere. Finally, the federation may be brought together as an escape from war. It must be kept together by conferring economic benefits which no state will desire to relinquish by secession; that it can confer such benefits need not be doubted.

The issue is one of the feeling of the nations when they come together in federation. It is better that they should federate for defence and foreign policy and equal access to their dependencies than not at all. They may come together more easily on a limited programme. But the further they can go in economic co-operation even at the outset, the stronger will be the bonds that will always unite them.

There will remain in any case a large field for national activity and distinctions, in education, health, social services and local administration, in forms and machinery of state government, in ways of living and ways of thought. In discussing the federation of nation-states it is natural to say most about those functions which might become federal. They have to be named because it is practically certain that division of powers in this case would follow the American and Australian precedents rather than the Canadian precedent; the federal authority would have defined powers while an undefined residue would be left to national authorities. But the ordinary citizen as a rule would be more conscious of the national than of the federal government.

Form of federal authority

In regard to the form of the federal authority, the framing of this is governed by two general considerations — that the individualities of the member states, large and small, must be adequately protected, and that the federal authority must be strong, with unquestioned power in its own sphere.

The first of these general considerations is important both for acceptance of federation at the outset, and for keeping it together in contentment. The purpose of federation is not the power of large nations but security for citizens of all nations and for their different cultures.

The second of these general considerations tells strongly against any plan of constituting a federal authority by nomination from national governments. Whatever provision were made for giving federal representatives a tenure independent of their nominators or securing that they should represent not simply the national party in power but all parties in fair proportion, it is difficult to believe that nominated federal representatives would ever have the authority that they will need. They cannot get this authority otherwise than directly from the people whom in common affairs they will govern. Whatever the difficulties of direct election, it seems essential that they should be overcome. Nor is there reason to suppose that they cannot be overcome, if the states for inclusion are chosen with this in mind.

This means, not only that the area of the federation must be manageable, but that every member state must be a democracy, with effective provision for peaceful change of governments and policies and for free discussion and association in parties. Requirement of democracy as a condition of federal membership results, not from abstract preference of democracy to dictatorship as a means of government, but from practical reasons. The working of a federal legislature as a super-national authority would become impossible if all the representatives of a particular nation were the nominees of one man: very rapidly it would become a cock-pit for national interests. Again, if it becomes impossible in any member state for the national government to be changed except by violence, the federal authority controlling the armed forces may be driven to an insoluble dilemma, between allowing disorder within the federation and supporting a dictator against a probable majority of his nationals. Effective democracy is a condition of federation.

These arguments point to a federal constitution on the following lines:

(a) A Federal Legislature of two Houses, one with membership based on population or electorate and chosen directly by the citizens, and one with equal or nearly equal representation of the separate states, whose members might be either elected or nominated by the national governments.

(b) A Federal Executive responsible to the Federal Legislature.

(c) A Federal Judicature interpreting a written constitution.

(d) Constitutional guarantees for the maintenance of effective democracy in each of the member states, i.e. for peaceful change of governments and policies in them by free discussion and association and secret voting.

These are the main lines only. To discuss all the constitutional problems of federation and the alternatives available for their solution would occupy many books, not part of a single pamphlet. The relations of the two Houses and possibility of deadlock between them, the methods of constituting the executive, the degree of responsibility of the federal authority for internal as well as external order, the delimitation of powers in respect of taxation or making treaties, the form in which the liberties essential to democracy shall be guaranteed in the constitution and the methods for making such guarantees effective, the provision for constitutional amendments — these and many other major problems arise as soon as federation becomes a practical issue. It is sufficient here to point out that federalism under a written constitution is not an uncharted field. Unfamiliar in Britain, its problems have been the subject of intense study and practical experiment for generations elsewhere. The problems have proved capable of solution, as they arose, in the existing federations. There is no reason to think of them as insoluble in a new federation.

FEDERALISM BY GENERAL APPROACH

The project of international federation set out above is based on a special approach to a particular manifestation of world disorder. It may be illustrated and supported by general considerations. How can the citizen obtain peace — security from external aggression as in any settled society he has security within his state? How can justice in place of war be established as the arbiter among nations?

One negative answer to the first question is clear and points to the positive answer of federation. The individual citizen cannot obtain security against external aggression by action limited to his own state. He cannot obtain peace from his fellow-citizens: he must seek it abroad. He cannot, it may be added, obtain peace from those who are already his friends abroad by turning alliance into union: peace must be won by going into the house of one's enemy and turning him into a friend. This is a special point leading to the particular federation proposed above — a union of belligerents. The main point is that the individual citizen can get internal order within his state, but must seek external order outside, by agreement with the individuals of other nations. He must have two governments: one for his internal national affairs, one for the common affair of securing peace with justice between men of his nation and those of other nations. That is federalism: for each citizen two governments, with a division of powers between them prescribed by a written constitution. The individual citizen can no longer be content to set up a national government and trust to that government either to defend him by its own strength, or to part with enough of its authority to a League of Nations that will defend him at need by collective strength. The national governments once having full sovereignty do not in practice part with it; they neither like to do so, nor feel justified in doing so, for they are trustees for their own nationals. The individual citizen, if he wants effective super-national government for world order, as well as a national government for internal order, must secure that the powers of government are divided from the start. Division of powers is federalism.

The answer to the second question points the same way. How can justice be established in place of war as the arbiter among nations, and secure the pacific settlement of international disputes? The obvious first step in answering that question is to ask how the same end is achieved in relation to individual disputes. The answer is that it is achieved on the one hand by reducing the force which any individual can control to insignificance as compared with the force at the back of justice, and on the other hand by establishing courts to say where justice lies.

In unsettled societies the individual relies upon his own strength for his security: each pioneer carries his musket. At a later stage he may supplement this by arrangements with particular neighbours for mutual defence. Later still comes the standing arrangement by which all members of a community agree beforehand to use their personal force in defence of any one of them and in punishment of a wrong-doer. Last of all comes the organisation of a permanent police force belonging to no individual and acting only on communal authority. Provision for individual security passes through four stages of self-defence, alliance, hue and cry, and the policeman; only with the last stage does security become assured; it is in practice assured most completely where the individual is disarmed most completely in favour of the state, while just dealing by the state itself is enforced by democracy.

Till twenty years ago, provision for the security of nations had not passed beyond the first or second stage: each nation relied on its own arms or sought to supplement them by alliance with particular neighbours. The failure of these methods is patent. Peace with justice among nations cannot be secured by the nations arming themselves or joining their arms in alliance with those of others. This is partly because the line between defensive and offensive armaments is unreal: the British Navy looks like a sure shield to the British, but looks a very different weapon to any other nation. It follows even more from inequalities in the size and strength of nations. The differences of strength between large and small nations are far greater than those between individuals or families. The unrestricted right of national armament today is patently inconsistent with small nations having any rights at all.

Peaceful settlement by justice of all disputes between nations can be made certain only on the same terms as those on which it is made certain among individuals, by making it impossible for any nation to challenge with any hope the force which justice automatically has at its command. This was the intention of the League of Nations Covenant. The war of 1914-18 led to a first experiment of adapting to international relations the device of hue and cry — the third stage in making security for the citizen. The Covenant of the League of Nations was designed, among other things, to provide collective security based on the armaments of individual nations. The failure of this experiment also is patent. This does not mean that the experiment of 1919 was not worth trying, or that any stronger measures would then have been accepted by the nations concerned. But it does suggest that a Covenant on the lines of that adopted in 1919 did not and probably cannot provide justice with force of the kind required, if justice is to rule among nations.

In the first place, the authors of the Covenant believed unduly in the compelling power upon nations of opinion among other nations. They spoke of public opinion as a force greater than any armaments. 'By far the strongest weapon we have is the weapon of public opinion.' 'What we rely upon is public opinion ... and if we are wrong about it, then the whole thing is wrong.'[49] On certain occasions, in the early days of the League, public opinion proved far from ineffective. But events have shown that it is not strong enough to be the strongest weapon of international order. 'The scales of Justice are vain without her sword.'[50]

In the second place, though the Covenant did not formally limit itself to public opinion as the force behind international justice, but contemplated more material sanctions, it relied upon individual nations to provide force for these sanctions by their own free will and from their national resources. This had three bad consequences:

(1) The power at the command of justice could not be great without making great also the power that might challenge justice. Potential wrong-doers had to provide the weapons for police-work.

(2) The policies of disarmament and of collective security came into conflict. Any of the major Powers — Britain or another — which implemented the fourth of the Fourteen Points and reduced its armaments to 'the lowest level consistent with domestic safety' unfitted itself thereby to be the sword of justice.

(3) The claims of justice and national policies of states supplying force came into conflict. No state would provide its national force to enforce a decision contrary to its own interests or in a way involving it in a war unpopular with its own nationals. And war as such was highly unpopular with the people of the states most devoted to the League of Nations.

Each of these weaknesses in turn has been illustrated in the last twenty years. It is hard to escape the conclusions drawn by Professor Carr, as to the nature of international power and the conditions of international government.

'Power is an indispensable instrument of government. To internationalise government in any real sense means to internationalise power; and since independent power is the basis of the nation-state, the internationalisation of power is really a contradiction in terms.

'Any real international government is impossible so long as power, which is an essential condition of government, is organised nationally.'[51]

The moral drawn here, though it does not appear to be drawn by Professor Carr himself, seems equally beyond question. Enforcement of justice by hue and cry, long abandoned as a means to internal order among citizens, is even less hopeful as a means of enforcing order among nations. To make war between nations impossible there is needed not an inter-national force, but a super-national force. Nations which really mean never to be at war again with one another, but are neither linked by indissoluble ties of blood or sympathy nor separated by unbridgeable distance must pool their arms in federation.

Federation comes when communities recognise a common interest for which it seems worth while to sacrifice something of their freedom to be separate. Today, in all material respects, the most distant countries named above for federation are closer than England and Scotland were at the time of their union, when it took ten or twelve days to journey from London to Edinburgh; when there was little trade, no telegraph, no broadcasting, no cycle of world depressions. Today the common interest of these and other countries in the preservation of peace is overwhelming.

THE LIMITS OF FEDERALISM

Federation has been proposed above for a limited area. Limitation of area is essential; federalism is a strong remedy for a virulent disorder; it is not a healing lotion that can be sprayed over the world. World federation is for the millennium. The federation projected here is for the next peace treaty: it is a federation of nations which from fresh experience of war will be determined to make as certain as they can that war will never be repeated.

If, in addition to the nations named above for inclusion, the United States of America desired to enter a Peace Federation, that would be a welcome revolutionary fact leading to readjustment of all plans. But that is too much to hope for and not necessary to the project here in view. World order, as distinct from European order, cannot be established without the co-operation of the United States of America. But the co-operation can take a form less intimate than federation with European states.

As regards the rest of Europe, the requirement of effective national democracy as a condition of federation would exclude automatically nearly the whole of it: Russia, Italy, Turkey, Spain, Portugal, and most of the Balkan States have Governments substantially autocratic.

The inclusion of Germany herself in the federation depends upon her return to democracy. There is no reason to think this unlikely if, with Hitlerism defeated, the democracies act promptly to keep Stalinism at bay. There is no reason, either, for democrats to be half-hearted in assertion of their principle. The doctrine of 1919 that making the world safe for democracy was the way to make it safe for all mankind was sound doctrine and remains so: the bitter laugh today is against those who derided it. The view that it is no concern of other nations what kind of government there is in Germany is academic theorising divorced from fact. If at the end of this war Germany cannot become democratic, the other nations of Europe will need to make themselves secure by military domination without partnership.

But there is no need to press democracy upon nations other than Germany. Their present Governments may be those which fit their present needs. They should not be tempted to change for the sake of joining the federation of Western democracies. Some of them may wish to form a different federation of their own, corresponding to their interests. The constitution of the Peace Federation would provide for accessions, but would not give a right of accession to any state that could satisfy formal requirements. Admission would depend upon the consent of the federation; and that consent might well be refused. A federation of north-western Europe and the British Dominions is manageable; once established it might be expected to grow in unity. Inclusion of other European countries, with different standards of life and with little or no experience of democracy, would weaken the federation and might end in revival of nationalist manoeuvres.

To some friends of federalism the suggestion that the area of federation must be limited strikes a chilling note. To some critics it appears a convenient handle for attack. The critics see in a selective federation an attack upon some other nation or some ideology. The friends feel that selection destroys the liberating virtue of a principle. The answer to friends and critics is the same, and in two stages. First, the boundaries suggested here for the Peace Federation are neither absolute nor final. They are those which, having regard to present conditions and prospective attitudes at the end of this war, seem most likely both to bring a federation into being and to enable it to function. Later revolutions in the minds of men may open the way to larger groupings. Second, some limitation of area, so far from taking the virtue out of the federal idea, is of its essence. Federalism is a principle which can be shared by all. A federation of nations is not a principle but a partnership. It is a partnership moreover of an active kind. Its analogy is not the co-operative store which any consumer who pays the subscription may join and which is strengthened by every new consumer. Its analogy is the co-operation of those who work together in a common task — of college or factory or family. Each working partnership must be based on compatibilities and must be selective for its purpose. But partnership is not exclusive. The closest partnership known — that of marriage — does not bar all other relations, with individuals or with other partnerships; those who enter this partnership do not thereby declare hostility to the rest of the human race.

Unquestionably any prospect of such a federation as that here projected would cause perturbation in some quarters, and raise questions for many peoples. Russia would see in it the end of her present adventures and in due course the loss of anything she might have gained. Italy would see in it a barrier to aspirations which she regards as legitimate. The United States and many other countries would be interested in its treatment of dependencies and in its economic policies.

It may be presumed that the federation itself will be peaceable. It will be too strong to fear attack from any other power, and will thus have no temptation to organise defensive war; it will have no reason to be jealous of voluntary association of other states or of full federation between them. It will be too varied in interests to be aggressive; it will have pacifism in its bones and disarmament as a natural goal. But the federation will have to be much more than peaceable in itself if it is to serve fully the cause of world order. 'The armed force of the Peace Federation shall be used to support justice among nations and to resist aggression wherever it may occur. The armed force of the Peace Federation shall not be used to gain for all or any of its members territory or economic advantage over any other state.' Declarations of this nature, though they could hardly be written into the constitution of the federation, should be deeply engraved in its policies from the start.

First, the federation should be prepared to use its armed forces in support of international justice throughout the world. In Europe no more than its own force would be needed. Outside Europe there is another focus of disorder — in Japan, China and Asiatic Russia. Here the federation could not act alone, but should be prepared to act for the restoration of order, in collaboration with the United States of America.

Second, as the federation should support justice against force throughout the world, so it should be prepared to accept justice in governing its own relation to other states. The federation will be acutely conscious of its own good faith and good intentions, but they may not always be obvious to others. It will not be easy for an immensely powerful association always to agree with others where justice lies, in its own cause. The acid test is likely to come over the treatment of dependencies in relation to the trading interests of other states.

For both the purposes named — to guide the use of the federation's force in maintaining international justice, and to allow the federation itself to accept justice in its own cause in place of its own decisions —

there is need for international machinery. Justice needs her scales as well as her sword. Without something in the nature of a World Council open to every state which recognises the interests of other states, without something in the nature of an Equity Tribunal, the Peace Federation outlined here cannot render its full service to the cause of world order. How these general organs of world order should be established and governed, how they should be related to existing institutions, how far they can be built on existing institutions, are themes for another discussion. But in one form or other they would surely be established if once the heart of Europe were healed and healthy.

The Peace Federation projected here is limited in area, so that it may be strong and real. The services which it may render to world order are not limited.

First, the federation can guarantee, as nothing else can, peace with justice within its area.

Second, the federation by its own strength can guarantee peace with justice in Europe. It is unlikely itself to be guilty of aggression, based as it will be on so many deeply pacific peoples with so great a variety of individual interests. It will be far too strong to be challenged by any European Power or any combination of such Powers. It can and should be prepared to guarantee the just rights of all the other nations in Europe, individually or grouped in federations.

Third, with peace in Europe guaranteed, it will be in a position to collaborate on equal terms with the peace-loving nations of America, in spreading peace with justice in the one part of the world that may still be a source of war and aggression, in the Far East to Europe and beyond the Far West of the United States.

THE NEXT STEP

A federation of the present belligerents and neighbour neutrals, if once it were established, might lead to peace with justice for all mankind. What is the chance of establishing it? On what does realisation of this dream of an ordered, secure, progressive world depend? On two things and two alone. The first condition is the defeat of Hitlerism in Germany — exorcism of the foul fiend that now possesses a great people. The second condition is that when Hitlerism has been exorcised, the people concerned — Britain, France and Germany first and others following them — should be willing to take those steps towards federal co-operation and limitation of national sovereignty which alone can secure them against return of war.

Will these two conditions in their turn be satisfied? No one today can answer that question. No one can say just in what circumstances the chance of making peace will come; with what balance of strength between the belligerents and with what parties to the war. The solid ground beneath our feet is being shaken by great forces. The coming year may hold events shattering to optimism; it may hold events that will make pessimism today look like shameful cowardice to-morrow.

But it is not only the future that is dark. No one can say today what is in the thoughts of the German people — those who to many in this country were once the most sympathetic and friendly nation other than our own. The hearts of these millions of human beings are dark to us. They cannot speak to us; we hear nothing but the braying of their masters. They cannot hear us, except by stealth. All that we know is that when last we were in communion with the German people, in September 1938, we thought that we recognised, in their acclamation of the delusive settlement at Munich, a peaceful spirit to match our own, and a desire equal to our own to avoid the horror and the shame of war.

Whether we were right or wrong, the deafening of German ears is not so complete as the gag upon their voices; though we cannot hear them at all, it is not wholly impossible for them to hear us. It is worth our while therefore to avoid saying those things which cannot but strengthen them in desperate support of their present rulers. They are being told that their troubles before the new war were due to the injustice of the Allies at Versailles; that the Allies, if victorious, will impose conditions yet more shameful than those of Versailles; that the very existence of the German people is at stake. In so far as they believe this, we strengthen their belief by talk of destroying the unity of Germany, by talk of such terms of peace as we should never accept for ourselves while we had a man left to fight or a gun to fire. What we ought to say to them is rather this:

'If and so long as you support the claim of your rulers that German might is the sole measure of German right, then the fight must continue until you change your minds; the tangible evidence of changed minds will be abandonment of the conquests which you have just made by force in Poland and in Czecho-Slovakia, and the giving of freedom to Austria to decide her own fate. If, however, you are already of that better mind, if you cause us to believe, as we should like to believe, that you are content to live in your own lands as we do in ours, respecting the rights of other nations, then we are ready to confer with you as to the means by

*which together you and we can meet three common needs. The
first is the need to make war between you and ourselves impossible
for ever; our plan is to pool your arms and ours in federation; if
you have another plan as effective for the purpose we will consider
it. The second is the need to deprive you of all sense of injustice;
our plan is that you with others should share with us those
economic advantages in colonial lands which you think are
unfairly ours. The third is the need to increase the prosperity and
security of your lives and ours; our plan is to join with you and
others in seeking solutions of the common economic problems of
mankind. One thing more we have to say. We mean that this time
the war shall end when it does end; there shall be nothing again of
what you have been taught to call the blockade which followed the
Armistice of 1918; once you have repaired the damage of your
recent conquests, there shall be no reparations. On the day that
fighting stops there shall, if we have our way, come into action an
International Reconstruction Commission charged with the duties
of relieving distress, repairing war damages and re-establishing
prosperity for all at the common charge of all. We hope to forge in
that the first link of our lasting equal union.'*

That is what we should try to say to the German people. In the view
of the British people the peace for which they are fighting is a peace of
fair-play for citizens of all nations; it is a peace against which the
German people would not wish to fight, if they understood it. To
persuade the German people of this is the only short cut to end the war
— the charm which might save millions of lives.

But the channels of persuasion are nearly blocked. The hearts of
the German people are dark to us and their ears are all but closed. To
those who are not belligerents, and to our allies and ourselves, we can
speak. As regards the neutrals, it is worth while to persuade them that
whatever may be our success in the war, we desire and will take nothing
from success but a gain that we can share equally with all mankind—
peace with justice in an ordered world; that ending this war we shall be
prepared to unite with them and others in constructive tasks of peace. If
the greatest of the neutral nations should come to feel that, in this age of
brigand empires and oppression of the weak, it is good to have a giant's
strength, but wrong to keep a giant's strength locked up for self-defence,
then that nation would become, as she is not yet, the Hope of the World;
man's struggle for freedom would be shortened; hundreds of thousands

of the youth of all nations now in conflict would live, who otherwise in the next years will die.

To our allies we can speak with the frankness of indissoluble friendship. The French see some things more clearly than the British do; the British see some things more clearly than the French do; true perspective needs a combination of views from different angles. Whatever our allies think, we want to know. What we say to ourselves, we say to them.

Among ourselves our task is by free discussion to fill in, line by line, a picture of the world that we should like to see after the war. By discussion we may convince ourselves that the world, if we take the right steps, can be a world without war. That in itself would be a potent aid to realising the first condition of this dream — to success in the present war. For success will depend first and foremost upon maintaining the spirit of the common people in France and in the British Commonwealth.

There is no doubt of the determination with which the British, in Britain and overseas, have turned from passionate desire for peace to acceptance of war. The final words of the Prime Minister's speech in announcing war could not be bettered as a statement of the feeling which has led us to this point; we have set out to fight what appear to us evil things — 'brute force, bad faith, injustice, oppression and persecution'. But while a negative reason of fighting evil may be sufficient for the beginning of a war, something else may be needed when determination comes to be tested by tribulation, by exhaustion, by fears of defeat. Then may be required the hope that at the end of war, not merely will evil be destroyed, but something good, something worth dying for and worth killing for, will be established. Only that hope sustained us from the frustration of 1916 to the victory of 1918. Only that hope can bring us with certainty to the same opportunity again. During this war, as early as we can, we must make a positive plan for the world that is to follow the war. The negative virtue of hating Hitlerism does not suffice.

Our plan for the world must be positive; it must also be new. The defeat of the high expectation of 1919, that war was finally banished from the world, was shattering and has left many even of those who go without question today to fight, without the hope which inspired those who fought a generation ago. They can and should be made to hope: the fact that the world failed once is not a reason for assuming that it will fail again in finding the way to end war. But hope will not return to the spell of old catchwords and general phrases. We must convince ourselves, old and young, that we have both a positive plan and a new plan.

Finally, the plan must be one that commends itself to the willing acceptance of our people and the others concerned. There can be no reasonable doubt that such a plan as that outlined above could work if it had the support of the peoples for whom it was established. Neither that nor any other scheme for world order can work which has not that support. Federation across national boundaries is both a positive plan and a new plan. All that remains is to see whether it is a plan that commends itself to the nations.

The title of this paper is a question: Peace by Federation? The mark of interrogation does not imply doubt that the federation here proposed, if once it were established by the wishes of the peoples concerned, would bring lasting peace to them, and lay the foundations of peace throughout the world; the federation would grow in unity and strength, solving each practical problem as it arose. The mark of interrogation stands because there are two other questions to which the answer is less certain. Will the peoples concerned be prepared to accept a plan of this kind? Is there any other plan which they would accept that would be as likely to achieve order in the world? The answer to the second question in my view is probably but not certainly 'No'. The answer to the first question, in my view, is probably but not certainly 'Yes'. I believe that when the issue is raised the peoples concerned will be prepared to barter arms for security and sovereignty for civilisation.

But there is no way of answering this question finally except by asking it and inviting discussion among the people themselves. Federation of kindred nations will work if they desire it. It will not work as a plan thrust on them by their rulers. To persuade the people of this country and of her allies and of other countries to choose this plan for themselves is the object of this paper. That is the next step.

Federation across national boundaries is a plan so new that it will be rejected by some critics as Utopian. If by Utopian these critics mean to describe a plan based on desires divorced from realities, then the plan is not Utopian. Whether the project outlined here be right or wrong, it starts from reality. It is based on facts: on the general fact of secular changes in the scientific and material equipment of mankind, making out of date old tribal groupings and isolations; upon two special revolutionary facts — of the unification of Germany and of aggressive Communism in Russia. These facts between them have changed the conditions of peace in Europe and the forms of government required there.

If, on the other hand, the term Utopian implies the vision of a world different from the world we live in, then the term describes literally the proposal of this paper. The plan of this paper is Utopian, for it aims at making a world different from the world that we have known for nearly a generation. The plan dares and needs to be Utopian because the choice is no longer between Utopia and the pleasant, ordered world that our fathers knew. The choice is between Utopia and Hell.

Robbins on a Federal Framework for an International Economy

Introductory Note

Lionel Robbins (1898-1984, later Lord Robbins) became a Professor of economics at the London School of Economics in 1929 when still only thirty years old, thus joining the brilliant group of social scientists, including a number of notable federalists, assembled there by Beveridge during his eighteen years as Director. Robbins remained at the LSE for the next thirty two years, apart from 1941-45 when he was Director of the Economic Section of the Offices of the War Cabinet. After leaving the LSE in 1961, he served for a decade as Chairman of the *Financial Times*. From 1961 to 1964 he was Chairman of the Committee on Higher Education, whose report led to the great expansion of higher education in the 1960s and proposed the end of the binary system separating polytechnics from universities, which was finally accomplished in the 1990s. A highly cultured man, he was also a Trustee of the National Gallery and the Tate Gallery, and a Director of the Royal Opera House, Covent Garden.

For his ideas on the need for a federal framework for the international and European economy Robbins acknowledged the contribution of Edwin Cannan, a predecessor as professor of economics at the LSE, who had already in World War One envisaged that when it was won the allies should found a federation together with the defeated powers, and who had also criticised the failure of free trade economists to realise that a liberal international economy required international institutions of law and government just as did a liberal economy within an existing state. Robbins developed this concept in his two remarkable books, *Economic Planning and International Order* (1937) and *The Economic Causes of*

War (1939), from which extracts are given below. The books were based on two series of lectures that he had been invited by Professor Rappard to give at the Institut Universitaire de Hautes Etudes Internationales in Geneva. The first analysed the reasons why the international economy needed the rule of law, both for certainty in such matters as contract, property and freedom of trade and for security in a more general sense, and went on to show that not only international courts but also legislative and administrative institutions were required: in short, a federal system of government.

In the spring of 1939, when he delivered the second series of lectures, Robbins was concerned to rebut the marxist theory that capitalism was the cause of war, by showing that war was a result of the absolute sovereignty of states and that, since state ownership and control of the economy as a whole involved the state in all economic disputes, socialism as practised by the communists was more likely than capitalism, with its pluralist character, to lead to war. It was not capitalism, but the system of sovereign states that had to be abolished. Through the summer, while the lectures were being written up into a book, war in Europe loomed ever closer; and when he wrote the final section in September 1939, World War Two had begun. The economic analysis of the two books went to the heart of a general political crisis, which had erupted in Europe rather than the wider international system. Robbins, not only a liberal economist but a man of profoundly liberal political values, made the concluding section of *The Economic Causes of War* an eloquent plea for the creation, after the war, of a federation of European democracies, including a democratic post-war Germany.

These two books were the most-cited sources in the two essays that Spinelli wrote on Ventotene and could, had the war not turned their minds in other directions, have helped the British to come more readily to terms with the political implications of the modern European and international economy. After completing the second book and before he went to the War Cabinet's secretariat in 1941, Robbins was an active contributor to the work of the Federal Union Research Institute. He wrote a report on 'Economic Aspects of the Federal Constitution' for its economic committee as well as a Federal Tract on *Economic Aspects of Federation*. The latter, the second in the series initiated with Beveridge's Tract reproduced above, was published for the Institute by Macmillans in 1941.[52] In his Tract Robbins advocated a federal union with free trade among the member states, free movement of people and capital, and a single currency: similar to the powers of the European Union today, but in the context of fully democratic federal institutions.

The first of the two extracts that follow is a section from *Economic Planning and International Order*, in which Robbins defined planning broadly as 'an attempt to shape means to ends', the end he had in mind being a liberal international economy; and he demonstrated the need for international law and government as a framework for this. The second extract comprises the concluding pages of *The Economic Causes of War*, in which he passionately advocated a European federation in order to ensure not only the framework for the liberal economy but also permanent peace among the member states after the war was won.

J.P.

A federal government for a liberal international economy *

by Lionel Robbins

... [I]f the term planning is *by definition* to be restricted to the operations of a centralised control, then the institutions of international liberalism are indeed excluded. The principle of international liberalism is decentralisation and control by the market. If we say that the term plan must not be applied to an organisation in which free initiative is guided to the service of free choice by an impersonal mechanism, then we have settled a point of terminology. But we have not judged the significance of the organisation. But the terminology is surely unfortunate. The essence of a plan is that it is an attempt to shape means to ends. In a world of change the essence of a successful plan of productive organisation is that it should bring about continual adaptation to changing technical conditions and changing demands of consumers. Now the various plans which we have examined hitherto do not do this. They involve a paralysis of the mechanism of adaptation: they tend to make the plan the end and the frustration of the consumers the means. They involve a tendency to a curtailment of productivity in a world which is certainly not over-burdened with plenty. Surely it is wise to attempt to avoid this kind of plan, to attempt to erect a world order which is capable of adaptation and which provides incentives to adaptation. It is this which is the object of international liberalism. It is an institutional pattern especially designed

---

* *Editor's note*. The following is an extract from Lionel Robbins, *Economic Planning and International Order* (London: Macmillan, 1937), pp. 224-46. The text is complete, save that footnotes have been omitted which relate to contemporary academic controversies. The text has been translated into Italian in Lionel Robbins, *Il federalismo e l'ordine economico internazionale*, with Introduction by Guido Montani (Bologna: Il Mulino, 1985), pp. 57-71.

to meet the difficulties of economic organisation on an international scale. If planning is an attempt to create institutions conducive to the satisfaction of the citizens, then international liberalism is a plan.

It is a plan, too, in the sense that it is to be the creation of government.

It is often held that liberalism denies all functions to government. The naïve belief that unguided self-interest is necessarily conducive to public benefit is thought to be the foundation of the liberal social philosophy: and a system which is held to rest upon such a superstition is, not unnaturally, condemned without examination.

For this belief the liberals of the past are not altogether blameless. It is, of course, a grotesque libel to suggest that men such as Hume, Adam Smith or Bentham regarded government as superfluous. To attribute to the great utilitarian philosophers the jejune presuppositions of an anarchistic philosophy of society can only be regarded as propagandist rhetoric. But it may be true that, in their preoccupation with the discovery of the laws of the market, they were apt sometimes to take the market itself for granted. It may be true too that, in their zeal to expose the results of interference with the disposal of property, they may have laid insufficient emphasis upon the framework of law and order which made the institution of property possible. In this way they, and still more the politicians who simplified their analysis for popular consumption, laid themselves open to misunderstanding and misrepresentation.

But, notwithstanding all that has been said to the contrary, it is a gross misconception to suppose that government and governmental bodies do not play a most important and indispensable role in the liberal plan of co-operation. To emphasise this is not to claim any additional virtue for the plan. In spite of certain contemporary habits of speech, there is no intrinsic virtue either in government or the absence of government: the totalitarian calculus weighs governmental and non-governmental actions indifferently. It is only to draw attention to an aspect of the plan, failure to understand which may lead to total misconception of the whole system. The characteristic institutions of a liberal society are inconceivable without government.

It should be obvious that they are inconceivable without security. If there is no authority armed with coercive power, the plans of the different citizens must be to some extent self-frustrating. They must provide for an apparatus of defence. This is necessarily wasteful; and it is often itself provocative. They must be short-run plans: it is not worth while planning for a long run of great uncertainty. Even so they are liable to continual disturbance. There can be no world-wide division of labour, no extensive accumulation, no elaborate organisation of production if arbitrary force is not restrained by force which is stronger but which is not arbitrary.

But this is not enough. The mere absence of violence is not a sufficient condition for the efficient working of free enterprise. For co-operation to be effective it must be restrained within suitable limits by a framework of institutions. Neither property nor contract are in any sense natural. They are essentially the creation of law; and they are not simple creations. For purposes of exposition, we may sometimes speak as if property rights and the system of contract were homogeneous and simple. But if we allow ourselves to be led into supposing that this is anything but the crudest of simplifications we fall into gross error. The system of legal rights in any existing society is a matter of the utmost complexity, the actual result of centuries of legislation and judicial decision. To determine wherein these rights are to consist if they are to be conducive to the satisfaction of the public choice, to delimit their scope and their content, is a task of the utmost difficulty. In what objects are property rights to be recognised? Are they to cover ideas and inventions? Or are they to be limited to source material resources and their utilisation? If so, what type of utilisation? May a man use his property in ways which mean damage to others? If not, how is damage to be defined? Are contracts to restrict trade permissible? If so, in what circumstances? If not, what is the definition of restriction? It is in the solution of questions of this sort that the task of legal planning consists. It is in the reference of particular cases to such a system of norms that the plans thus made are continually translated into practice. The system of rights and duties of the ideal liberal society may be thought to be a good plan or it may be thought to be a bad plan. But to describe it as no plan is not to understand it at all. The idea of a co-ordination of human activities by means of a system of impersonal rules, within which what spontaneous relations arise are conducive to mutual benefit, is a conception, at least as subtle, at least as ambitious, as the conception of prescribing positively each action or each type of action by a central planning authority: and it is perhaps not less in harmony with the requirements of a spiritually sound society. We may blame the enthusiasts who, in their interest in what happens in the market, have paid too little attention to its necessary framework. But what shall we say of those who argue perpetually as if this framework did not exist.[53]

But this is not all. The provision of security and a suitable legal system is a function more important and more complex than is often suspected. But it does not exhaust the province of government. The market apparatus has its limits: and outside these limits arise certain generally acknowledged wants which, if they are not satisfied by governmental action, will either not be satisfied at all or, at best, will be satisfied very inadequately.

It is not possible or desirable exhaustively to enumerate such cases. But it is not difficult to describe their general nature. On the one hand, there exist wants which must be satisfied collectively or not satisfied at all. Of this class provision against infectious diseases is a conspicuous instance. It is comparatively useless for the individual to make private provision here. He may be willing to pay all that is technically necessary. But unless all others are doing likewise his expenditure may be ineffective. On the other hand, there arise wants which can be formulated individually, but for whose supply spontaneous contracts between private property owners is not effective. Of this class the demand for certain means of communication is typical. It is possible for individuals to offer money for means of access to different places. But, in many cases, in the absence of government action in some shape or form the supply will not be forthcoming. It is not inconceivable that an extensive road system should be satisfactorily created by private enterprise. But it is not probable: and, if it is not, then there may be need for another kind of plan.

This necessity has long been recognised. Adam Smith made it the third of his list of duties of the sovereign 'to erect and maintain certain public works and certain public institutions which it can never be to the interest of any individual or small group of individuals to maintain.'[54] But in recent years it has become more important. The development of technique has brought it about that many services of obvious utility are best rendered by methods which involve the use of a network of long strips of land difficult to establish save by compulsory acquisition — rail transport and canals, drainage, water supply, electricity, telegraphic and telephonic communication, and so on. It is not certain that the supply of these services is best organised on the basis of governmental or quasi-governmental monopoly. Current discussion of the matter is usually interested or superficial: the task of independent scrutiny of the most suitable institutions here has scarcely yet begun. But it is certain that, in some form or other, governmental action is necessary. It is certain, too, that the field of such necessary action is extensive.

If this reasoning is correct, it is therefore wrong to regard the proposals of international liberalism as involving no plan. On the contrary, they constitute the one plan we have so far examined which does not at once display conspicuous internal weakness when conceived on a world scale.

It would be equally wrong to regard them as a plan which has ever yet been realised. Much of the order which exists even at the present owes its origin to private enterprise and the market. If there were no markets and no private enterprise our position would be even worse than it is. It is indeed one of the strongest recommendations of liberal institutions that their vitality as organising influences is displayed even on the smallest scale and in the most adverse circumstances. But, as our earlier investigations have shown, the world today is not predominantly liberal. It is nationalist and interventionist; and the continual succession of political and economic catastrophes which this involves gives what market mechanism exists a task which no mechanism can perform. It is not liberal institutions but the absence of such institutions which is responsible for the chaos of today.

Indeed, if we preserve a sense of perspective, the conspicuous fact that emerges from any historical survey is radically different from what the reactionaries — both fascist and communist — endeavour to make us believe. International liberalism is not a plan that has been tried and failed. It is a plan that has never yet had a full chance. The chaos of today is not something new. It is a relapse to what hitherto has been the normal condition of the human race. The difference between the economic organisation of today and the economic organisation of the past is great. But it is a difference of scale and technical process and potentialities for world-wide disaster. The principles have been the same. They have been sectional, monopolist, restrictionist. The results too have been similar. There has been poverty and insecurity. There was little freedom of enterprise before the nineteenth century. There were close corporations, state monopolies, restrictions on movement, sectional trade agreements, prohibition, tariffs... . Only in the middle of the eighteenth century did men begin even to conceive of a world in which privilege to restrict should be restricted and in which the disposition of resources should obey, not the demands of producers for monopoly, but the demands of consumers for wealth.

For a short time it seemed as if this dream might be realised. When Adam Smith wrote *The Wealth of Nations* it seemed to him that to expect the establishment of complete freedom of trade in Great Britain was 'as absurd as to expect that an Oceana or Utopia should ever be established in it'.[55] But the power of ideas operating in a milieu of favourable political accidents was stronger than even he suspected. In thirty years he had made converts of the great majority of educated Englishmen. By the middle of the nineteenth century, the Corn Laws had been repealed, restrictions on movement abolished and what to all intents and purposes were the beginnings of a liberal economic system established in Great Britain.

The influence of these changes was not confined to Great Britain. The internal policy of the United States of America, although lacking much in power to control the excesses of the frontier spirit, was predominantly liberal. And for a brief period indeed it seemed as if the countries of the European mainland would develop similar institutions. From the forties to the seventies of the nineteenth century the trend of legislation almost everywhere was liberal. Tariffs were lowered. Personal unfreedom was abolished. Enterprise was freed. Monopolies were dissolved. International division of labour was extended. And the consequential increase of wealth was spectacular.

But reaction was not long in asserting itself. From the seventies onwards the tide began to flow in the opposite direction. In Central and Eastern Europe the ideas of international liberalism had never taken firm root. The idea that production could be organised without the existence of an organiser who gave orders, as Frederick William gave orders to his guards, was not easily assimilated by minds few of which had ever really thrown off the habits of intellectual sycophancy of autocratic courts. The failure of the '48 and the unification of Germany by Blood and Iron created an atmosphere in which the principles of mercantilism were once more respectable. The Physiocrats were condemned: the Cameralists exalted. The systems of List and Schmoller took the place of the system of Smith and Ricardo. Neither the socialists on the left nor the conservatives on the right, each only the representatives of special interests, ever grasped the view that co-operation without regulation from the centre could be anything other than chaos. The reimposition of the iron and steel duties by Bismarck at the end of the seventies, and his explicit adoption of the principles of imperialism, were the death-knell of liberalism in Germany. The practice of the totalitarian Third Reich is only the practice of Bismarckian Germany writ large.

There were other influences tending in the same direction. In its origins socialism, equally with liberalism, was rationalist and utilitarian.

It rested on the belief, clearly susceptible of reasonable discussion, that there was a technique of economic organisation superior to a system of free enterprise. But early efforts to demonstrate this were not successful; and the attempt was soon abandoned. With the decline of the French Utopians, socialism relapsed into the messianic mysticism of Marxian determinism; or it allied itself with the special interests of trade-union restrictionism. Its propaganda, although professedly international, had the effect of weakening belief in the free market and strengthening the movement for the revival of national controls. It thus played directly into the hands of the reaction. The nationalist reactionaries well knew how to steal the thunder of the socialists and present it in a 'more human', 'more practicable' form.

Nor must the mistakes of the liberal reformers be left out of the picture here. There is no doubt that the early liberals had not thought out completely the implications of their position. They were weak on the problem of associations, and they did not really grasp the problem of national sovereignties. In consequence, they sometimes followed policies which created new opportunities for privilege and emphasised national differences: and at every step the representatives of special interests were alert to exploit their blunders. The dictatorship of the consumer is a drastic purge of inefficiency: and those sections of the community whose privileges were menaced were not over-scrupulous about their methods of defence.

But when all this is taken into account, it is the nationalist reaction which must claim the main credit for arresting the liberal revolution. The claim of Hitler to have saved Europe from Marx and Lenin may be dubious. But Bismarck certainly 'saved' us from Cobden and Adam Smith. In the history of the last sixty years it is the influence of German thought and German policy which has been dominant. The existence, at the centre of European civilisation, of a Power whose statesmen and thinkers openly rejected liberalism and regarded the atavistic ideals of imperialism as the be-all and end-all of policy, exercised an influence which it is difficult to exaggerate. It gave the tone to thought and legislation even in countries where liberalism persisted. British imperialism was made in Germany, and the paternalism of the official liberal party in Great Britain was modelled on Bismarck's 'Social State'. It dominated foreign policy. It accentuated national divisions and international alliances. And in the end it brought about the Great War in which liberal institutions began to founder and in whose aftermath they have been nearly swept away.

International liberalism is not a plan which has been tried and failed. It is a plan which has never been carried through — a revolution crushed by reaction ere it had time to be fully tested.

We can see this all the more vividly if we try to sketch out for ourselves some of the changes which are necessary to make international liberalism a reality. To imagine that, in the present state of opinion, these changes will come about may be as absurd as to imagine the establishment of an Oceana or a Utopia. But it is always useful to know the significance of different directions of movement. And if we have found that other plans lead to institutions which seem to be ultimately unworkable, it is, at least, interesting to know whether this plan would be doomed to frustration for similar reasons.

We do not have to look far before coming to the main requirement. According to the outline of the functions of government which we have already made, the first essential is security. There cannot be an orderly international division of labour, there cannot exist the complicated network of financial and economic relations essential to the proper development of the earth's resources, if the citizens are continually in danger of violence. In the present state of technique as regards communications and production, this is more important than it ever has been. Without order, no economy; without peace, no welfare.

But it is in just this most elementary requirement of a comprehensive international plan that our present organisation is most conspicuously lacking. There is world economy. But there is no world polity. The different national states each arm against the other. Between their members there is not the ordered freedom of the liberal state but the brutish anarchy of the state of nature. The opportunities of division of labour make us members one of another. But for lack of proper governmental machinery we make war or prepare for war continually. We should regard it as absurd if the inhabitants of the county of London maintained armed forces for defence against the inhabitants of the surrounding counties and the inhabitants of surrounding counties maintained armed forces against them. We should regard it as childish, atavistic, wasteful, if not actually productive of chaos. Yet, because of the division of the world into national units, similar arrangements between areas, equally interdependent and equally indistinguishable by any criteria other than the arbitrary heritage of past governmental arrangements, are not merely taken for granted as inevitable but even regarded as contributing to the general good. These are no doubt matters of ultimate valuation. Whether it is a good thing or a bad thing to kill without judicial process is a question which, even at the present day, is often decided differently according to the nationality of the victims. But this thing is certain. The nationalistic anarchy is wasteful. Whatever value we may put on the military virtues as such, there can be no doubt that, at the present time, the existence of this apparatus for eliciting such virtues is more costly, in terms of the other things we have to sacrifice, than any other luxury the human race affords. How much misery might have been avoided, how much poverty prevented, had the accident of history not divided the seat of sovereignty.

It is just here that we can perceive one of the main deficiencies of nineteenth-century liberalism. It was the great achievement of the men of those days to have realised the harmony of interest of the inhabitants of different national areas. But they did not sufficiently realise that the achievement of this harmony was only possible within a framework of international security, They thought that if they demonstrated the wastefulness and futility of economic and political warfare it was enough. If each national state were limited to the performance of the functions proper to a liberal government there would be no occasion for international conflict. There would he no need for a supernational authority.

But this was a grave error. The harmony of interests which they perceived to be established by the institutions of property and the market necessitated, as they had demonstrated, an apparatus for maintaining law and order. But whereas *within* national areas such an apparatus, however imperfect, existed, *between* national areas there was no apparatus at all. Within the national areas they relied upon the coercive power of the state to provide the restraints which harmonised the interests of the different individuals. Between the areas they relied only upon demonstration of common interest and the futility of violence: their outlook here, that is to say, was implicitly not liberal but anarchist. But the anarchist position is untenable. It is true that, for the citizen who does not love war as such, abstention from violence is an obvious matter of self-interest. It is true that, in the long run, aggression seldom pays the aggressor, and that even victory is associated with impoverishment. But if we are not content to rely on such arguments for the preservation of order within the nation, we have no reason to believe that such reliance would be effective in preserving international order.

Es kann der Beste nicht in Frieden leben
Wenn es dem bösen Nachtbar nicht gefällt.

The existence of *one* state whose leaders have evil intentions can frustrate the co-operation of a world of peaceful peoples. It is not by the demonstration that burglary and gangsterdom do not pay, that we restrain the activities of burglars and gangsters: it is by the maintenance of a mechanism of restraint. And it will not be without a mechanism of restraint that international burglary and gangsterdom are banished from the face of the earth.[56]

'A man must be far gone in Utopian speculations who can seriously doubt that if ... states ... be wholly disunited or only united in partial confederacies, the subdivisions into which they might be thrown would have frequent and violent contests with each other. To presume a want of motive for such contests as an argument against their existence would be to forget that men are ambitious, vindictive and rapacious. To look for a continuation of harmony between a number of independent, unconnected sovereignties in the same neighbourhood would be to disregard the uniform course of human events, and to set at defiance the accumulated experience of ages.'[57]

But how is the apparatus of restraint to be provided?

It is becoming very obvious that mere associations of sovereign states are ineffective. The confederation — the *Staatenbund* — has never been very successful: and in our own day its weaknesses are only too painfully evident. So long as the different states retain their sovereignty, so long can decrees against them be enforced ultimately only by armed alliances of other states. Every word that was written by the founders of the American constitution against the confederal form of government has been vindicated again in our own time by the history of the League of Nations.

'Government', wrote Hamilton, 'implies the power of making laws. It is essential to the idea of law that it be attended with a sanction.... If there be no penalty attached to disobedience, the resolutions or commands which pretend to be laws will, in fact, amount to nothing more than advice or recommendation. This penalty, whatever it may be, can only be inflicted in two ways: by the agency of the courts and ministers of justice, or by military force: by the COERCION of the magistracy, or by the COERCION of arms. The first kind can evidently apply only to men: the last kind must of necessity be employed against bodies politic or communities or states. It is evident that there is no process of a court by which the observance of the laws can in the last resort be enforced. Sentences may be denounced against them for violations of their duty: but these sentences can only be carried into execution by the sword. ...

'In every political association which is formed upon the principle of uniting in a common interest a number of lesser sovereignties, there will be found a kind of eccentric tendency in the subordinate or inferior ones by the operation of which there will be a perpetual effort in each to fly off from the common centre. ...'[58]

Only the surrender of sovereignty, of the right to make war, by the national governments can remove the danger.

But a completely unitary world state is neither workable nor desirable. Its unworkability depends essentially upon the extent of the area and the complexity of the language conditions over which it would have jurisdiction. We have seen this difficulty in surveying the possibilities of international communism. It would arise even in a completely liberal system. For a central authority to be responsible for roads and public health both in Austria and Australia would be absurd. Nor could we be sure that such a body would be an efficient safeguard of liberty. Caligula once wished that the whole Roman people could be united in one head so that at a single blow he might have the supreme ecstasy of decapitating it. That great Leviathan, the unitary world state, might present similar temptations to our modern sadists. If independent sovereignty is chaos, the unrestricted unitary state might be death.

There is only one solution to this stupendous problem. The first need of the world is not economic but political revolution. It is not necessary that a world state should have powers unrestricted by constitution. But it is necessary that the national states should surrender certain rights to an international authority. The right of making war and the power to do so must be given up. But they need not give up all their rights of independent government; and the rights of the international authority must also be limited. There must be neither alliance nor complete unification, but Federation; neither *Staatenbund*, nor *Einheitsstaat*, but *Bundesstaat*.

Here we once more see the far-reaching wisdom of the founders of the American constitution. They did not produce a perfect constitution. Perfection of political arrangements is not to be hoped for, is indeed not even conceivable. It is obvious that both in the American Federation which exists and in any world or smaller federation which might be modelled on it, there remain great problems of providing for proper adaptation of the division of federal and state powers and adjusting the areas of regional administration. No sane person will pretend that the American constitution today provides an instrument which is at all perfectly adapted to the necessities of government under present technical conditions. But when all these obvious deficiencies are taken into account, the fact remains that they did construct an instrument which has reconciled the interests of a multitude of people over vast stretches of the earth's surface and has created an area of peace and internal freedom for economic co-operation which is without precedent in history. They did establish a principle which offers the one hope of escape from the fear of destruction which today overshadows humanity. And when we contrast the peace and the riches of that great Union with the chaos and anarchy of the unhappy nations of Europe we know that this was something worth doing, worth preserving, worth fighting to preserve. We can read Abraham Lincoln's noble dedication of the dead at Gettysburg and know that his claims were just.

...

The need for a
European federation *

by Lionel Robbins

The root cause of international conflict

... The ultimate condition giving rise to those clashes of national economic interest which lead to international war is the existence of independent national sovereignties. Not capitalism, but the anarchic political organisation of the world is the root disease of our civilisation.

Against this, however, it might be argued that such conflicts are not necessary. If the different sovereign states would abstain from the practices of restrictionism, if their citizens would banish from their hearts the desire for sectional advantage, these things need not happen. Rightly interpreted, the long-run interests of the inhabitants of the different national areas are not in disharmony. Whatever the prospects of momentary advantage from restrictionist manipulation and aggression, in the modern world at least, the long-run interests of all who are not sadistic maniacs lie above all in the preservation of peace.

Such was the belief of the Cobdenite liberals, in spite of the jeers of the uneducated, probably the most disinterested body of men who ever influenced the policy of a great nation. But, in spite of its nobility, it was grounded in error. It is true that, rightly interpreted, the long-run interests of the majority of the human race are not in conflict. It is true that, for humane men, the disaster of war is an evil of the first order of magnitude. But it is not true that, in the absence of the rule of law, there is any security against its occurrence. The Cobdenite liberals would have never dreamt of urging that, within national areas, the long-run interests of the majority in peaceful co-operation could be regarded as secured without a framework of law and coercion. Such a view would have been the view, not of liberals, but of philosophical anarchists. What justification had they, therefore, for assuming that, in the relations between the

---

* *Editor's note*: The following extract comprises the final section of Lionel Robbins, *The Economic Causes of War* (London: Jonathan Cape, 1939), pp. 99-109, translated into Italian in Robbins, op. cit. (note 9, p.125 below), pp. 179-89.

inhabitants of different national areas, a superior harmony might be expected? If they did not expect the mere demonstration of long-run interest, unsupported by law, to secure an absence of anti-social behaviour *within* the nation, why should they have expected that it would do so *between* nations, where the play of irrational prejudice and the lack of understanding and sympathy were so much more likely to be prevalent?[59] Surely the truth is that, if the different national governments are free to do anything, there is a strong probability that, with the best will in the world on the part of the majority, from time to time, error or sinister interest will result in policies leading to disharmony.

We can see this very plainly if we turn for a moment from the relations of geographical groups to the relations of groups of producers. It is possible to argue that, rightly interpreted, the interests of different groups of producers are not in long-period disharmony. If one group alone restricts output, it is quite possible that it may gain; but if all groups play the same game, then most at least will be the poorer.

Nevertheless, knowledge of such long-period harmonies does not justify us in believing that, if groups of producers are given by statute a position of uncontrolled monopolistic privilege, the prospect of short-period gain will not tempt them very often to abuse it. It is true that governments have sometimes acted on this assumption and that the 'experts' they have consulted have done nothing to warn them of its dangers. But experience shows that it is unwarranted. If groups of producers are given positions of monopolistic privilege, a state of affairs is created in which the emergence of policies tending to disharmony can be regarded as almost inevitable.

In exactly the same way, if geographical groups have uncontrolled powers of restriction and exclusion, if there is no framework of law limiting the actions of independent sovereign states, then a state of affairs exists in which the abuse of these powers is probable. There exists a state of affairs in which the delusions of restrictionism and the sinister influence of the pressure groups have scope and effectiveness — a state of affairs in which the deep-seated non-rational impulses of nationalism have the maximum opportunity to become entangled in the support of economic policies which ultimately lead to war. However true it may be that in the long run such policies can be shown to lead to impoverishment and international conflict, there is no reason to suppose that, in the absence of the restraints of a rule of law, the majority of the citizens will be sufficiently alert or sufficiently long sighted to prevent their emergence. A world organisation which depends upon the continual dominance in every sovereign state of the principles of Cobdenite liberalism, is an organisation which is bound not infrequently to be disorganised. The dominance in one important state or group of states of different principles is liable to endanger the whole system. A system of sovereign geographical groups is no less likely to be provocative of clashes of interest than a system of 'sovereign' groups of producers.

All this becomes very clear if we take a hypothetical example, which, but for the foresight of a small group of men and the courage and consistency of their successors, might easily have become an example in actual history.

Under the constitution of the United States of America, the governments of the different states are prohibited from imposing protective tariffs on imports or exports. They are prohibited from limiting migration or the movement of capital. All these matters are the prerogative of the federal government.

Let us suppose that things had been different. Suppose that the Constitutional Congress had broken down and there had eventually arisen, in that great area, instead of one federation, forty-eight independent sovereign states.

Does any man of experience doubt for a moment that there would have arisen also, in America as in Europe, a network of restriction on interstate economic relations? Trade would have been limited. The interests in various states would have protested against the 'flood of cheap imports'; even under the present constitution there are formidable barriers in the shape of spurious veterinary regulations and such-like measures not guarded against by the founders of the constitution.[60] Migration would have been hampered. If prosperity in one part was greater than in another, there would have been protests against the 'flood of immigrant labour'; in the recent depression, unconstitutional limitations of this sort have actually been attempted by various states. Relations of debtors and creditors would have been endangered. If the states of the middle west were depressed, not only would there be isolated failures to keep faith with eastern creditors, there would also be imposed the paralysing apparatus of exchange control and partial repudiation with which European practice has made us familiar. And the result of all this would be interstate conflict. The different governments would feel it incumbent on them to maintain national power by alliances and manoeuvres. The inhabitants of the poorer states would covet the privileges of the richer states. There would be talk of the necessity for *Lebensraum*. Where debt was repudiated, the cause of the investors might become a matter of diplomatic friction; it is easy to imagine an expeditionary force from New York invading, let us say, Kansas to protect the interests of the bond-holders.

In short, we should be confronted with the whole dreary spectacle of power politics with its manoeuvres, its devotions, its mass sentiment, and its background of sinister interest, with which the history of unhappy Europe has made us so depressingly familiar. And the pacifists would say that it was due to lack of virtue. The biologists would say it was an aspect of the inevitable struggle for existence. The psychologists would say it was a manifestation of the death instinct which it would take a thousand years research to learn to sublimate.[61] The Marxians would say it was all due to the capitalist system. And certain among the historians would hint that it was the result of dark subtle forces of which only they understood the mystery.

But in fact, it would be due to the existence of independent sovereign states. No doubt it would be possible to investigate further the catastrophe which had brought it about that this, rather than federation, had been the line of evolution. If Hamilton had not lived or if Lincoln had faltered .... or if the economic interests of dissenting states had succeeded in securing the rejection of the proposals of the Constitutional Congress — any of these things might have caused the path of history to be different. But in the sense in which cause may be said to be a condition in the absence of which subsequent events could not have happened, the existence of independent sovereign states ought be justly regarded as the fundamental cause of conflict. And since we know that it was deliberately to avoid such a state of chaos that Hamilton and his friends devised the existing constitution, we may well regard their motives as the cause of its freedom from this kind of embarrassment. In the sense which is significant for political action, it is the chaos of independent sovereignties which is the ultimate condition of international conflict. It is not only because the independent states have the power to declare war, that war is sometimes declared, it is also because they have the power to adopt policies involving clashes of national interest of which war seems the only solution.

The United States of Europe

If this is so, then the remedy is plain. Independent sovereignty must be limited. As citizens of the various national states, we may hope to diminish the danger of conflict by opposing policies which tend to evoke it. But this is not enough. The apparatus of modern war is so formidable, the cost of its maintenance so onerous, the dangers of actual conflict are so great, that we cannot afford to rely on spontaneous goodwill as our only safeguard against catastrophe. There must be an international framework of law and order, supported by solid sanctions which prevent the emergence of those policies which are eventually responsible for conflict. We do not need a unitary world state; such an organisation would be neither practicable nor desirable. But we do need a federal organisation; not a mere confederation of sovereign states as was the League of Nations, but a genuine federation which takes over from the states of which it is composed, those powers which engender conflict. The founders of the League of Nations were right in that they recognised the need of a supernational authority; their error was that they did not go far enough. They did not realise that the effective functioning of a supernational authority is incompatible with independent national sovereignty. But today we know this. The history of the League of Nations is one long demonstration of the truth of the proposition long ago set forth by Hamilton and Madison, that there is no safety in confederations. We know to-day that unless we destroy the sovereign state, the sovereign state will destroy us.[62]

Now, of course, it is quite Utopian to hope for the formation in our time of a federation of world dimensions. There is not sufficient feeling of a common citizenship. There is as yet no sufficiently generalised culture. In present conditions, even the electoral problems of such a body would present insurmountable difficulties. The formation of a world system, the political consummation of the unity of the human race, may well be regarded as the divine event towards which all that is good in the heritage of the diverse civilisations of the world invites us to strive. But, whatever we may hope for in the distant future of the planet, it must be clear that, at the present stage of human development, any attempt at so comprehensive an organisation would be necessarily doomed to disaster.

But it is not Utopian to hope for the construction of more limited federations — for the merging of independent sovereignties in areas where there exists the consciousness of a common civilisation and a need for greater unity. In particular it is not Utopian to hope for the formation of a structure of this kind in that part of the world now most menaced by the contradictions of its present political organisation — among the warring sovereignties of Europe.[63] So far is it from being Utopian that, for those with eyes to see, it is the most urgent practical necessity of the age.

For it is surely plain that the present political organisation of Europe has completely outlived its usefulness and is now nothing but a menace to the very existence of the civilisation it has helped to bring forth. When the sovereign states of modern Europe emerged from the feudalism of the middle ages, their functions were liberalising and creative. They eliminated the mass of local restrictions which were strangling economic development. They pacified the warring barons and princes and established uniformity of law over areas given over to particularism. But, at the present time, it is, not their unifying, but their separatist tendencies which have become dominant. They restrict the activities of an economic life which, in its spontaneous development, spreads far beyond their borders. They are uneconomic units for the administration of what positive functions they discharge; and the burden of maintaining the apparatus of defence which is necessary to secure their independence, threatens more and more to absorb all the energies of their inhabitants. The existence of restrictions to trade and movement between the different states of Europe today is as absurd as the existence of similar restrictions between different provinces at earlier periods. To an intelligent outsider unacquainted with the background of our history, the maintenance of vast armies by the states of Europe for defence against each other must be hardly less ridiculous than would be the maintenance of armies for the separate defence of the towns or departments within these states. The system has reached breaking point; and, with the development of modern military techniques, it has no longer survival value. As gunpowder rendered obsolete the feudal system, so the aeroplane renders obsolete the system of the independent sovereignties of Europe. A more comprehensive type of organisation is inevitable. Will it come by mutual agreement or by caesarian conquest? That is the unsolved question. For either there must be empire or federation; on a long view, there is no alternative.

But to create such a federation will not be easy. We have a common culture. But we have no common language. We have a common history. But it is riven by fratricidal quarrels. No one who has realised the nature of the interests involved in the perpetuation of the present powers of the independent sovereign states can be blind to the strength of the opposition to any attempt to eliminate our disunity. The federation of the thirteen secession states of the new world was almost wrecked by local particularism, even though they were united by a common tongue, common habits and the memory of recent action against a common enemy. How much harder must it be for the warring states of Europe, with none of these aids, to establish a basis of unity. It will not be easy to make the new Europe.

Nevertheless, of all the tasks which present themselves to our generation, it is that which is most worth while attempting. The age in which we live is an age in which men have worshipped many idols and followed many false visions. It has seen nationalism run mad and collectivism turn oppressor. The ideals of the romantic rebellion have proved dead sea fruit in our hands. But the great ideals of liberty, justice and mutual tolerance and the heritage of art and learning which is their spiritual outcome, have not been found wanting. The more they have become endangered, the more important we have discovered them to be. But it is just these things which are in peril from the disunity of Europe. The political structure amid which they have developed has developed stresses and strains which threaten to overwhelm them; if they are to be preserved, a constructive effort is necessary. Not merely because war is terrible, not merely because it impoverishes, but because it threatens all that is most valuable in the cultural heritage of Europe, we must devise institutions which banish it from our midst. It is because the civilisation of Socrates and Spinoza, of Shakespeare and Beethoven, Michelangelo and Rembrandt, of Newton and Pascal, is at stake that we must build a new Europe.

And now that the war has come and our hopes of peaceful developments lie shattered, this necessity is all the greater if the end is not to be chaos. We are fighting Germans. If European civilisation is not to perish, we must destroy the tyranny which rules over them. No one with any sense of history and art will deny the existence of a real German problem in Europe — the incapacity for self-government, the tendency to brutality and sadism, the fascination with the death motive, the moral clumsiness, the deep sense of spiritual insecurity, which again and again, since the rise of Prussia, have been a menace to the peace and liberties of Europe. But for all that, Germans are Europeans. They are part of our civilisation; and Europe can never be completely healthy till Germany is healthy too. Somehow or other we must create a framework in which the German *Geist* can give its best, not its worst, to Europe. A draconian peace will do nothing. The Nazis must be extirpated; but we have neither the strength nor the will to keep Germans in subjection for ever. What more appropriate outcome of our present agonies, therefore, what more fitting consecration of the blood which is being shed, than a peace in which this great people, purged of its devils, shall be coerced into free and equal citizenship of the United States of Europe?

Spinelli on Ventotene

Introductory Note

In 1924, two years after Mussolini had seized power, Altiero Spinelli (1907-86), just seventeen years old, entered both the law faculty of the University of Rome and the young communists' organisation. Three years later he was arrested and spent the next sixteen years incarcerated by the fascist regime, ten years in prison and six years confined in prison camps. While in prison he read widely and, impressed by non-marxist writers and resenting the straitjacket of communist doctrine, he challenged the party line and was expelled in 1937. In 1939, in confinement on the island of Ventotene, he met Ernesto Rossi, a professor of economics who had been imprisoned as a leader of the social-liberal organisation Giustizia e Libertà and who had been inspired in particular by the British liberal tradition. After reading articles by the liberal economist, Luigi Einaudi, advocating a European federation, they studied works by contemporary British federalist writers, including Lionel Robbins and others whose ideas were synthesised in the text by William Beveridge, reproduced above. These ideas had such an impact on Spinelli that he devoted the rest of his life to the federalist cause.

Spinelli and Rossi wrote the Ventotene Manifesto in order to initiate a movement to campaign for a European federation; and Spinelli, while still on Ventotene, wrote two essays on the subject. On being liberated from Ventotene in 1943, Spinelli initiated the foundation of the Italian federalist movement, which he was to lead as its secretary general from 1948 to 1962, and took steps towards the creation of the Union of European Federalists. He campaigned for a constituent assembly to draw up a federal European constitution, playing an influential part in the project for a European Political Community which was abandoned together with the European Defence Community in 1954; and he then, rejecting Jean Monnet's approach of building up the European Community by stages through the Treaties of Rome, launched a campaign for a Congress of the European People, intended itself to organise elections for a constituent assembly. After this too failed, he devoted most of the 1960s to academic activities, teaching at the Bologna Center of the Johns Hopkins University and founding the Istituto Affari Internazionali in Rome. In 1970 he entered the Community institutions for the first time, as a member of the European Commission. In 1976, he was elected to the Italian Chamber of Deputies and became one of its representatives in the European Parliament, then still indirectly elected.

Spinelli was elected a Member of the European Parliament in the first direct elections to the Parliament in 1979 and set about persuading his fellow MEPs to initiate a process of revising the Community treaties, as a step towards a federal constitution. He secured the establishment of the Committee for Institutional Affairs, of which he became the general rapporteur. He then organised the Committee's work to such effect that it produced a Draft Treaty for European Union which, thanks to his intensive efforts to secure the support of the main party groups, the Parliament adopted by a massive majority in February 1984. The Draft Treaty was supported by the Belgian, Dutch, German and Italian Parliaments and also by the responsible organs of the French parliament and, crucially, by President Mitterrand. Although its main elements were opposed by the British, Danish and Greek governments, the Draft Treaty was one of the impulses leading to the Single European Act and to its provisions for enhancing the role of the Parliament. Spinelli was bitterly disappointed that this result was so much more modest than the Draft Treaty which was the crowning achievement of his long years of federalist struggle. He did not live to see how the Single Act relaunched the Community, leading on to, among other things, the single currency and further strengthening of the Parliament.

Of the two texts reproduced below, the Ventotene Manifesto was written in 1941, most of it by Spinelli in consultation with Rossi, who contributed a section on economic and social policy. The Manifesto analysed the fundamental political problem that would face a post-war Europe of sovereign nation-states, affirmed that it could be solved in the context of a European federation and proposed the foundation of a federalist movement to campaign for this. Written as it was in one of Mussolini's prison camps, parts of the Manifesto were coloured by the existence of the fascist states in Germany and Italy and the need for their transition to become democratic participants in a European federation, together with the assumption that the federation must be created in a 'revolutionary situation' immediately after the end of the war. These parts are not relevant to the questions facing member states of the European Union today and some have been omitted from the text below. Spinelli analysed them in greater detail in his essay, also reproduced below, on 'The United States of Europe and the Various Political Tendencies'. Written in the year following the Manifesto, this text benefited from Spinelli's further reflections on the federalist project and the relationship with it of democrats, of communists and of nazi racists. He provided a compelling critique of the incompatibility of communist and fascist doctrines with the project of a democratic federation and, while he was yet to acquire first-hand knowledge of the workings of liberal democracies, a penetrating analysis of the forces likely to support the establishment of a European federation and then to sustain it. Part of Rossi's contribution, also overtaken by the events of the past half-century, has likewise been omitted and is summarised on pages 10-11 above.

J.P.

The Ventotene Manifesto *

by Altiero Spinelli and Ernesto Rossi

I. THE CRISIS OF MODERN CIVILISATION

Modem civilisation has taken the principle of freedom as its basis, a principle which holds that man must not be a mere instrument to be used by others but an autonomous centre of life. With this principle at hand, all those aspects of society that have not respected it have been placed on trial, a great historical trial.

1) The equal right of all nations to organise themselves into independent states has been established. Every people, defined by its ethnic, geographical, linguistic and historical characteristics, was expected to find the instrument best suited to its needs within a state organisation created according to its own specific concept of political life, and with no outside intervention. The ideology of national independence was a powerful stimulus to progress. It helped overcome narrow-minded parochialism and created a much wider feeling of solidarity against foreign oppression. It eliminated many obstacles hindering the free movement of people and goods. Within the territory of each new state, it brought the institutions and systems of the more advanced societies to more backward ones. But with this ideology came the seeds of capitalist imperialism which our own generation has seen mushroom to the point

---

* *Editor's note:* Originally published in Rome in 1944 in A.S. e E.R., *Problemi della Federazione Europea* (Roma: Movimento Italiano per la Federazione Europea), reprinted in Spinelli - Rossi, *Il Manifesto di Ventotene* (Napoli: Guida editori, 1982), and published in English in Altiero Spinelli - Ernesto Rossi, *The Ventotene Manifesto* (Ventotene: The Altiero Spinelli Institute for Federalist Studies, 1988).

where totalitarian states have grown up and world wars have been unleashed.[*]

Thus the nation is no longer viewed as the historical product of co-existence between men who, as the result of a lengthy historical process, have acquired greater unity in their customs and aspirations and who see their state as being the most effective means of organising collective life within the context of all human society. Rather the nation has become a divine entity, an organism which must only consider its own existence, its own development, without the least regard for the damage that others may suffer from this. ... As a consequence, from being the guardian of citizens' freedom, the state has been turned into a master of vassals bound into servitude, and has all the powers it needs to achieve the maximum war efficiency. Even during peacetime, considered to be pauses during which to prepare for subsequent, inevitable wars, the will of the military class now holds sway over the will of the civilian class in many countries, making it increasingly difficult to operate free political systems. Schools, science, production, administrative bodies are mainly directed towards increasing military strength. Women are considered merely as producers of soldiers and are rewarded on the basis of the same criteria as prolific cattle. From the very earliest age, children are taught to handle weapons and hate foreigners. Individual freedom is reduced to nothing since everyone is part of the military establishment and constantly called on to serve in the armed forces. Repeated wars force men to abandon families, jobs, property, and even lay down their lives for goals, the value of which no-one really understands. It takes just a few days to destroy the results of decades of common effort to increase the general well-being.

Totalitarian states are precisely those which have unified all their forces in the most coherent way, by implementing the greatest possible degree of centralisation and autarky....

2) The equal right of all citizens to participate in the process of determining the state's will is well established. This process should be the synthesis of the freely expressed and changing economic and ideological needs of all social classes. A political organisation of this kind made it possible to correct or at least minimise many of the most glaring injustices inherited

---

* *Editor's note*. Writing two years later Spinelli, citing Robbins's *The Economic Causes of War*, repudiated the marxist theory that imperialism was a direct consequence of capitalism ('Politica marxista e politica federalista', *in Il Manifesto di Ventotene*, op.cit., p.103).

from previous regimes. But freedom of the press, freedom of assembly, and the steady extension of suffrage, made it increasingly difficult to defend old privileges, while maintaining a representative system of government.

Bit by bit those without property learned to use these instruments to fight for the rights acquired by the wealthy. Taxes on unearned income and inheritances, higher taxes levied on larger incomes, tax exemptions for low incomes and essential goods, free public schooling, greater social security spending, land reforms, inspection of factories and manufacturing plants were all achievements that threatened the privileged classes in their well-fortified citadels.

Even the privileged classes who agreed with equality in political rights could not accept the fact that the underprivileged could use it to achieve a de facto equality that would have created a very real freedom with a very concrete content. When the threat became all too serious at the end of the First World War, it was only natural that these privileged classes should have warmly welcomed and supported the rise of dictatorships that removed their adversaries' legislative weapons.... Subsequently totalitarian regimes consolidated the position of the various social categories at the levels they had gradually achieved. By using the police to control every aspect of each citizen's life, and by violently silencing all dissenting voices, these regimes barred all legal possibility of further correction in the state of affairs.... In order to keep the working classes immobilised and subjugated, the trade unions, once free and militant organisations, run by individuals who enjoyed the trust of their members, have been turned into institutions for police surveillance run by employees chosen by the ruling class and responsible only to them. Where improvements are made in this economic regime, they are always solely dictated by military needs which have merged with the reactionary aspirations of the privileged classes in giving rise to and consolidating totalitarian states.

3) The permanent value of the spirit of criticism has been asserted against authoritarian dogmatism. Everything that is affirmed must prove its worth or disappear. The greatest achievements of human society in every field are due to the scientific method that lies behind this unfettered approach. But this spiritual freedom has not survived the crisis created by totalitarian states. New dogmas to be accepted as articles of faith or simply hypocritically are advancing in all fields of knowledge.

Although nobody knows what a race is, and the most elementary understanding of history brings home the absurdity of the statement, physiologists are asked to believe, demonstrate and even persuade us that people belong to a chosen race, merely because imperialism needs this myth to stir the masses to hate and pride. The most self-evident concepts of economic science have to be treated as anathema so as to enable autarkic policy, trade balances and other old chestnuts of mercantilism to be presented as extraordinary discoveries of our times. Because of the economic interdependence of the entire world, the living space required by any people which wants to maintain a living standard consistent with modern civilisation can only be the entire world. But the pseudo-science of geopolitics has been created in an attempt to prove the soundness of theories about living space and to provide a theoretical cloak to the imperialist desire to dominate.

Essential historical facts are falsified, in the interests of the ruling classes. Libraries and bookshops are purged of all works not considered to be orthodox. The shadows of obscurantism once more threaten to suffocate the human spirit. The social ethic of freedom and equality has itself been undermined. Men are no longer considered free citizens who can use the state to achieve collective goals. They are, instead, servants of the state, which decides what their goals must be, and the will of those who hold power becomes the will of the state. Men are no longer subjects with civil rights, but are instead arranged hierarchically and are expected to obey their superiors without argument, the hierarchy culminating in a suitably deified leader. The regime based on castes is reborn from its own ashes, as domineering as it was before.

After triumphing in a series of countries, this reactionary, totalitarian civilisation has finally found in Nazi Germany the power considered strong enough to take the last step. After meticulous preparation, boldly and unscrupulously exploiting the rivalries, egoism and stupidity of others, dragging in its path other European vassal states, primarily Italy, and allying itself with Japan, which follows the very same goals in Asia, Nazi Germany has launched itself on the task of crushing other countries. Its victory would mean the definitive consolidation of totalitarianism in the world. All its characteristics would be aggravated to the utmost degree, and progressive forces would be condemned for many years to the role of simple negative opposition.

The traditional arrogance and intransigence of the German military classes can give us an idea of the nature of their dominance after victory in war. The victorious Germans might even concede a facade of generosity towards other European peoples, formally respecting their territories and their political institutions, and thus be able to command while at the same time satisfying the false patriotic sentiments of those who count the colour of the flag flying at the country's borders and the nationality of prominent politicians as being the major considerations and who fail to appreciate the significance of power relationships and the real content of the state's institutions. However camouflaged, the reality is always the same: a new division of humanity into Spartans and Helots.

Even a compromise solution between the two warring sides would be one more step forward for totalitarianism. All those countries which managed to escape Germany's grasp would be forced to adopt the very same forms of political organisation to be adequately prepared for the continuation of hostilities.

But the very fact that Hitler's Germany has managed to chop down the smaller states one by one has forced increasingly powerful forces to join battle. The courageous fighting spirit of Great Britain, even at that most critical moment when it was left to face the enemy alone, meant that the Germans came up against the brave resistance of the Russian Army, and gave America the time it needed to mobilise its boundless productive resources. This struggle against German imperialism is closely linked to the Chinese people's struggles against Japanese imperialism.

Huge masses of men and wealth are already drawn up against totalitarian powers whose strength has reached its peak and can now only gradually consume itself. The forces that oppose them have, on the other hand, already survived the worst and their strength is increasing.

With every day that passes, the war the allies are fighting rekindles the yearning for freedom, even in those countries which have succumbed to violence and have lost their way as result of the blow they received. It has even rekindled this yearning among the peoples in the Axis countries who realise they have been dragged down into a desperate situation, simply to satisfy their rulers' lust for power.

The slow process which led huge masses of men to be meekly shaped by the new regime, who adjusted to it and even contributed to its consolidation, has been halted and the reverse process has started. All the progressive forces can be found in this huge wave which is slowly gathering momentum: the most enlightened groups of the working classes who have not let themselves be swayed, either by terror or by flattery, from their ambition to achieve a better standard of living; the sharpest members of the intellectual classes, offended by the degradation to which intelligence is subjected; entrepreneurs who, wanting to undertake new initiatives, want to free themselves of the trappings of bureaucracy and national autarky, which bog down all their efforts; and finally, all those who, with an innate sense of dignity, will not bend an inch when faced with the humiliation of servitude.

Today, the salvation of our civilisation is entrusted to these forces.

II. POST-WAR TASKS: EUROPEAN UNITY

Germany's defeat would not automatically lead to the reorganisation of Europe in accordance with our ideal of civilisation.

In the brief, intense period of general crisis (when the states will lie broken, when the masses will be anxiously waiting for a new message, like molten matter, red-hot, and easily shaped into new moulds capable of accommodating the guidance of serious internationalist-minded men), the most privileged classes in the old national systems will attempt, by underhand or violent methods, to dampen the wave of internationalist feelings and passions and will ostentatiously begin to reconstruct the old state institutions. Most probably, the British leaders, perhaps in agreement with the Americans, will try to push things in this direction, in order to restore balance-of-power politics....

The revolutionary situation: old and new trends

The fall of the totalitarian regimes will, in the feelings of entire populations, mean the coming of 'freedom'; all restrictions will disappear and, automatically, very wide freedom of speech and assembly will reign supreme. It will be the triumph of democratic beliefs. These tendencies have countless shades and nuances, stretching from very conservative liberalism to socialism and anarchy. These beliefs place their trust in the 'spontaneous generation' of events and institutions and the absolute goodness of impulses originating among the grass roots. They do not want to force the hand of 'history', or 'the people', or 'the proletariat', or whatever other name they give their God. They hope for the end of dictatorships, conceiving this as restoring the people's unsuppressible right to self-determination. Their crowning dream is a constituent assembly, elected by the broadest suffrage, which scrupulously respects the rights of the electors, who must decide upon the constitution they want. If the population is immature, the constitution will not be a good one, but to amend it will be possible only through constant efforts of persuasion. ... As the democrats wear down their initial popularity as assertors of freedom by their endless polemic, and in the absence of any serious political and social revolution, the pre-totalitarian political institutions will inevitably come to be reconstituted, and the struggle will again develop along the lines of the old class opposition.

The principle whereby the class struggle is the condition to which all political problems are reduced has become the fundamental guideline of factory workers in particular. It gave consistency to their politics for as long as the fundamental institutions were not questioned. But this approach becomes an instrument which isolates the proletariat, when the need to transform the entire social organisation becomes paramount. The workers, brought up in the class system, cannot see beyond the demands of their particular class or even their professional category and fail to concern themselves with how their interests link up with those of other social classes. Or they aspire to a unilateral dictatorship of the proletariat in order to achieve the utopian collectivisation of all the material means of production, indicated by centuries of propaganda as the panacea for all evils. This policy attracts no class other than the workers, who thus deprive the other progressive forces of their support, or alternatively leaves them at the mercy of reactionary forces which skilfully organise them so as to break up the proletarian movement.

Among the various proletarian tendencies, followers of class politics and collectivist ideals, the communists have recognised the difficulty of obtaining a sufficient following to assure victory so that, unlike the other popular parties, they have turned themselves into a rigidly disciplined movement, exploiting the Russian myth in order to organise the workers, but which accepts no orders from the workers and uses them in all kinds of political manoeuvrings.

This attitude makes the communists, during revolutionary crises, more efficient than the democrats. But their ability to maintain the workers as far removed from the other revolutionary forces as they can, by preaching that their 'real' revolution is yet to come, turns them into a sectarian element that weakens the sum of the progressive forces at the decisive moment. Besides this, their absolute dependence upon the Russian state, which has repeatedly used them in pursuing its national policies, prevents this Party from undertaking political activity with any continuity. They always need to hide behind a Karoly, a Blum, a Negrin, only to fall headlong into ruin together with the democratic puppets they used, since power is achieved and maintained, not simply through cunning but with the ability to respond fully and viably to the needs of modern society. ... The most probable result would be that the reactionaries would benefit more than anyone else. ... The reactionary forces have capable men and officers who have been trained to command and who will fight tenaciously to preserve their supremacy. ... They will certainly be the most dangerous force to be faced.

The point they will seek to exploit is the restoration of the nation-state. Thus they will be able to latch on to what is by far the most widespread of popular feelings, so deeply offended by recent events and so easily manipulated to reactionary ends: patriotic feeling. In this way they can also hope to confound their adversaries' ideas more easily, since for the popular masses, the only political experience acquired to date has been within the national context. It is, therefore, fairly easy to channel them and their more shortsighted leaders towards the reconstruction of the states destroyed in the storm.

If this end is achieved, the forces of reaction will have won. In appearance, these states might well be largely democratic and socialist. But it would only be a question of time before power fell into the hands of the reactionaries. ... The question which must be resolved first, failing which progress is no more than mere appearance, is the definitive abolition of the division of Europe into national, sovereign states. The collapse of the majority of the states on the Continent under the German steam-roller has already given the people of Europe a common destiny: either they will all submit to Hitler's dominion, or, after his fall, they will all enter a revolutionary crisis and thus will not find themselves separated by, and entrenched in, solid state structures. Feelings today are already far more disposed than they were in the past to accept a federal reorganisation of Europe. The harsh experience of recent decades has opened the eyes even of those who refused to see, and has brought to maturity many circumstances favourable to our ideal.

All reasonable men recognise that it is impossible to maintain a balance of power among European states with militarist Germany enjoying equal conditions with other countries, nor can Germany be broken up into pieces or held on a chain once it is conquered. We have seen a demonstration that no country within Europe can stay on the sidelines while the others battle: declarations of neutrality and non-aggression pacts come to naught. The uselessness, even harmfulness, of organisations like the League of Nations has been demonstrated: they claimed to guarantee international law without a military force capable of imposing their decisions and by respecting the absolute sovereignty of the member states. The principle of non-intervention turned out to be absurd: every population was supposed to be left free to choose the despotic government it thought best, in other words virtually assuming that the constitution of each individual state was not a question of vital interest for all the other European nations. The multiple problems which poison international life on the Continent have proved insoluble: tracing boundaries through areas inhabited by mixed populations, defence of alien minorities, weapons for landlocked countries, the Balkan Question, the Irish problem, and so on: all matters which would find easy solutions in the European federation, just as corresponding problems, suffered by the small states which became part of a vaster national unity, lost their harshness as they were turned into problems of relationships between various provinces.

Moreover, the end of the sense of security, inspired and created by an unassailable Great Britain, which led Britain to 'splendid isolation', the dissolution of the French army and the disintegration of the French Republic itself at the first serious collision with the German forces (which, it is to be hoped, will have lessened the chauvinistic attitude of absolute Gallic superiority), and in particular the awareness of the risk of total enslavement are all circumstances that will favour the constitution of a federal regime, which will bring an end to the current anarchy. ... And, once the horizon of the old Continent is superseded, and all the peoples who make up mankind are included in a single design, it will have to be recognised that the European federation is the only conceivable guarantee ensuring that relationships with American and Asian peoples will work on the basis of peaceful cooperation, waiting for a more distant future when the political unity of the entire world will become possible.

Therefore, the dividing line between progressive and reactionary parties no longer coincides with the formal lines of establishing more or less democracy, or the pursuit of more or less socialism, but the division falls along a very new substantial line: those who conceive the essential purpose and goal of struggle as being the ancient one, the conquest of national political power — and who, albeit involuntarily, play into the hands of reactionary forces, letting the incandescent lava of popular passions set in the old moulds, and thus allowing old absurdities to arise once again — and those who see the main purpose as the creation of a solid international state, who will direct popular forces towards this goal, and who, even if they were to win national power, would use it first and foremost as an instrument for achieving international unity. *

---

* *Editor's note.* Having observed the weakness of democracy in many European states in the inter-war period, leading to the replacement of many of them by authoritarian regimes, Spinelli's assumption here was that such weakness and eventual collapse would recur, whatever the precise nature of the democratic constitutions and policies established by the several nation-states after the war, unless they were united in a European federal democracy.

By means of propaganda and action, seeking to establish in every possible way agreements and links between the individual movements which are certainly in the process of being formed in the various countries, the foundations must be built now for a movement that knows how to mobilise all forces for the birth of the new body which will be the grandest creation, and the newest, that has occurred in Europe for centuries; that will constitute a steady federal state, with a European army at its disposal instead of national armies; that will break decisively economic autarkies, the backbone of totalitarian regimes; that will have sufficient means to see that its decisions for the maintenance of common order are executed in the individual federal states, while each state will retain the autonomy it needs for an articulation and development of political life moulded to the particular characteristics of the various peoples.

If a sufficient number of men in the main European countries understand this, then victory will soon fall into their hands, since both circumstances and opinion will be favourable to their efforts. They will have before them parties and factions that have already been disqualified by the disastrous experience of the last twenty years. Since it will be the moment for new action, it will also be the moment for new men: the MOVEMENT FOR A FREE AND UNITED EUROPE.

III. POST-WAR DUTIES: REFORM OF SOCIETY

A free and united Europe is the necessary premise to the strengthening of modem civilisation with regard to which the totalitarian era is only a temporary setback. As soon as this era ends the historical process of struggle against social inequalities and privileges will be restored in full. All the old conservative institutions that have hindered this process will either have collapsed or will be teetering on the verge of collapse. The crisis in these institutions must be boldly and decisively exploited.

In order to respond to our needs, the European revolution must be socialist, i.e. its goal must be the emancipation of the working classes and the creation of more humane conditions for them. The guiding light in determining what steps need to be taken, however, cannot simply be the utterly doctrinaire principle whereby private ownership of the material means of production must in principle be abolished and only temporarily tolerated when dispensing with it entirely. Wholesale nationalisation of the economy under state control was the first, utopian form taken by the working classes' concept of their freedom from the yoke of capitalism.

But when this state control is achieved, it does not produce the desired results but leads to a regime where the entire population is subservient to a restricted class of bureaucrats who run the economy.

The truly fundamental principle of socialism, vis-à-vis which general collectivisation was no more than a hurried and erroneous inference, is the principle which states that, far from dominating man, economic forces, like the forces of nature, should be subject to man, guided and controlled by him in the most rational way, so that the broadest strata of the population will not become their victims. The huge forces of progress that spring from individual interests must not be extinguished by the grey dullness of routine. Otherwise, the same insoluble problem will arise: how to stimulate the spirit of initiative using salary differentials and other provisions of the same kind. The forces of progress must be enhanced and extended, by giving them increasing opportunities for development and employment. At the same time, the tracks guiding these forces towards objectives of greatest benefit for all society must be strengthened and perfected. ...

These are the changes needed both to create very broad-based support around the new institutional system from a large number of citizens willing to defend its survival and to stamp freedom and a strong sense of social solidarity onto political life in a very marked way. Political freedom with these foundations will not just have a formal meaning but a real meaning for all since citizens will be independent, and will be sufficiently informed to be able to exert continuous and effective control over the ruling class.

It would be superfluous to dwell at length on constitutional institutions, not knowing at this stage, or being able to foresee, the circumstances under which they will be drawn up and will have to operate. We can do no more than repeat what everyone knows about the need for representative bodies, for the legislative process, for the independence of the judiciary (which will replace the present system) ensuring impartial application of the laws, and for the freedom of the press and right of assembly guaranteeing informed public opinion and the possibility for all citizens to participate effectively in the life of the state. ...

The federalist movement cannot be amateurishly improvised at the decisive moment, but must begin to be formed forthwith at least as regards its central political attitude, its upper echelons, the basic lines for action.* It must not be a heterogeneous mass of tendencies, united merely negatively and temporarily, i.e. united by their anti-Fascist past and the mere expectation of the fall of the totalitarian regime, in which all and sundry are ready to go their own separate ways once this goal has been reached. The movement, on the contrary, knows that only at this stage will its real work begin. It must therefore be made up of men who agree on the main issues for the future. ...

While overlooking no occasion or sector in which to spread its cause, it must be active first and foremost in those environments which are most significant as centres for the circulation of ideas and recruiting of combative men. It must be particularly active vis-à-vis the working class and intellectuals, the two social groups most sensitive, in the present situation, and most decisive for tomorrow's world. The first group is the one which submitted the least to the totalitarian rod and which will be the quickest to reorganise its ranks. The intellectuals, particularly the younger intellectuals, are the group which feels most spiritually suffocated and disgusted with the current despotism. Bit by bit other social groups will be drawn into the general movement. ... if the movement continues resolutely from the very outset to create the conditions required for individual freedom whereby every citizen can really participate in the state's life, it will evolve, notwithstanding secondary political crises, towards increasing understanding and acceptance of the new order by all — hence towards an increasing possibility of working effectively and creating free political institutions.

The time has now come to get rid of these old cumbersome burdens and to be ready for whatever turns up, usually so different from what was expected, to get rid of the inept among the old and create new energies among the young. Today, in an effort to begin shaping the outlines of the future, those who have understood the reasons for the current crisis in European civilisation, and who have therefore inherited the ideals of movements dedicated to raising the dignity of mankind, which were shipwrecked through either their inability to understand the goal to be pursued or the means by which to achieve it, have begun to seek each other out and to meet.

---

* *Editor's note.* The Manifesto, in referring to the federalist organisation that it envisaged, used both the terms 'movement' and 'revolutionary party', the latter reflecting the particular problem facing federalists under the fascist regime. Since this problem has been irrelevant in the EC/EU for over half a century, and since the term 'movement' is the more frequently employed in the Manifesto, it is the one used here.

The road to pursue is neither easy nor certain. But it must be followed and it will be!

The United States of Europe and the Various Political Tendencies *

by Altiero Spinelli

Wir gehören zum Geschlecht, das aus dem Dunkeln ins Helle strebt.
Goethe

The nature of the profound evil undermining European society is by now only too obvious to all: it is modern total warfare, the preparation and conduct of which employs all the social energies of any single country. When it breaks out, it destroys men and wealth; when it smoulders under the ashes, it is like an exhausting nightmare, oppressing all other activities. No-one today can consider it with the carefree attitude of former times. Some thirty years ago 'fresh and joyful war', the intoxicating, short and relatively cheap adventure, might have charmed the thoughtless, who had not reflected on the enormous destructive capacity of modern technology and on the barbarisation of minds. The men of today, who for the most part are seeing this scourge for the second time, know all the stupidity of this myth, and realise that the permanent danger of armed conflict between civilised peoples must be completely eradicated to prevent the destruction of all one holds most dear. It may be useful to indicate briefly the general orientation of ideas around this problem, and what one might reasonably expect from these orientations, if they should be realised in actual institutions and actions. We can group them, overlooking minor nuances, around three typical trends:

---

* *Editor's note.* Originally published in Rome in 1944 in A.S. e E.R., *Problemi della Federazione Europea*, op. cit., and reprinted in Spinelli - Rossi, *Il manifesto di Ventotene*, op.cit.

87

1) racism, which sees a solution in establishing the rule of the superior race;

2) democracy, which sees the cause of war in tyrannical regimes, and counts on peace necessarily accompanying the restoration of democracy;

3) communism, which blames conflict on capitalism and therefore calls for its abolition as the necessary condition for peace among peoples.

After examining these three trends we will try to indicate the road along which we must seek the solution most suited to the needs of European civilisation.

Racism and European unity

1) For the naïve European who, without much reflection, had believed nineteenth century civilisation to be, so to speak, the natural and spontaneous form in which human activity expresses itself, the emergence and massive growth of the racist attitude seems to be more or less an accumulation of absurdities, of madness, of falsity. In reality, respect for reciprocal freedom on the basis of legal equality is only the result of a complex historical process into which the actual immediate tendencies of the human mind have been channelled, directing them towards goals different from those to which they would spontaneously turn. Civilised man is a complicated and fragile product. The most magnificent fruits of civilisation are due to the iron discipline which the latter imposes on the barbarous human mind. Yet when men find themselves faced with problems whose solution is of vital importance and which they nevertheless fail to solve because of the resistance they encounter and the lack of instruments suited to solving them in a civilised way, that discipline can shatter and allow primordial forces to emerge. These tend to solve difficulties with the violent imposition of their will.

If these forces prevail, they tend to organise all of society according to the relationship of master and servant. The master decides autocratically what is to be done: the servant does what the master orders. Those who resist must be subjugated or, if they will not submit, destroyed. He who subjugates, thus affirms his personality, his demands. He who submits, thus renounces his own autonomy, and prefers to keep his own life by making it depend on another, rather than to lose it. This is the law intrinsic to the type of society based on the right of the strongest.

2) Over the centuries our civilisation had abolished the master-servant relationship in law, and was seeking ways to abolish it also in fact. Instead, it has reappeared from the depths to become dominant in unexpected forms. Elsewhere, one might examine the events leading to the re-emergence of this attitude in one country or another, affirming itself in its purest form in Germany. Here, it is enough to note that it was not caused, but merely occasioned, by economic motives, along with many others.

The great crises of the post-war period were among the greatest difficulties against which modern social discipline was shattered, providing an opening for the atavistic tendencies latent in the human mind. Once unleashed and asserted, this attitude of conquest becomes the centre of impulses and actions, resolving the problems facing it according to its innermost nature. In modern society, the master-servant relationship is realised in its most coherent form in German racism. The racist myth, however inconsistent it may be in the light of scientific knowledge, represents the ideal criterion by which to fix the hierarchy of values and work out the division of mankind into castes. All the political, social, economic and cultural energies which society had developed are transformed into instruments of the masters' control. The country is organised into a Spartan kind of racist collectivism: that is, a military organisation capable of holding firm the distinction between dominators and dominated, of avoiding divisions among the former and of exploiting the servants of inferior grade to the advantage of the masters and of higher grade servants, i.e. the so-called dominant people. The latter is in reality itself a docile instrument in the hands of the restricted castes that are the real rulers, and is used to subjugate other peoples. Lower grade servants below the Germans already include the Czechs, the Poles, the Jews, etc. Domination and the consequent right of exploitation reach wherever force can reach. No scruple towards others has any right to exist, since the others are by definition instruments or obstacles, servants or enemies.

3) The absurd anarchy of European international organisation is the most propitious terrain imaginable for the full expression of racism. The latter is certainly inclined to try to organise the continent and its colonial appendages as a field to be exploited by the master race. The contradictions arising from the existence of nation-states would no longer exist in such a case. For their solution would for a whole epoch be the exploitation and military colonialisation of all Europe to the advantage of a single national community. Speculation, whether about the legal or the economic forms

which this empire might assume, is absolutely devoid of importance. The exploitation could take on such collectivist aspects as imposing tributes on the subjugated communities, or such capitalist aspects as restrictive provisions to make the market function in the desired direction.

Whatever the further developments of this regime may be, it is certain that its victory would mean the establishment of a type of caste civilisation totally different from that towards which Europe has so far been developing. The Nazi orientation could be realised either intelligently or stupidly, but it is to be noted that the goals it proposes are not unachievable because of internal contradictions, and the means which it uses can also be coherent. One cannot therefore reasonably expect that it is destined to collapse because of inherent inconsistency. The profound significance of the present war, beyond the particular political and economic problems that it entails, is therefore not that of a war of economic imperialism, nor of a war of more or less domineering nations. It is that of a war of civilisations, waged in order to decide if our life should succumb or not to that atavistic resort. Whoever has some knowledge of the history of primitive peoples knows that this is their natural way of behaviour. The hesitation to apply these categories to today's events comes simply from the entirely unjustified opinion that the forms of barbaric civilisation are connected with a very low level of technical knowledge, and that they are therefore impossible today. In reality they are only connected with very elementary spiritual attitudes, and can co-exist perfectly well with aeroplanes and radio.

Democracy and European unity

1) Common experience shows that man, when he finds himself involved in a situation that upsets his traditional habits and presents new aspects, is very much inclined to ignore the new problem and rather to bring it back to the old, to reconstitute the old codes of behaviour, in which everything unfolded 'reasonably', calmly. The will which appears inclined towards creation is, on the contrary, almost always devoted to restoring the already known.

This attitude cannot be despised, since it is the foundation of continuity in the life of individuals and groups. Nothing could be seriously undertaken if people thought they could start at the beginning again each time. Normally one takes possession of a new experience by relating it to familiar motives and habits. But it is a tendency which becomes quite absurd, fed no longer on reason but on nostalgia, when it tends to pursue ends and apply means which, because of their nature and the circumstances in which they can now be realised, lead inevitably to the ruin of what one would wish to see consolidated. In order therefore to measure the positive or negative value of this tendency, it is necessary to examine the coherence of its ends and means.

The most typical example of this attitude in political life today is in the restoration of national democracy, which would see re-established the two principal foundations on which nineteenth century European civilisation rested and developed, and which the course of events has brought down. First, the principle according to which every nation has the right to organise itself into an absolutely independent sovereign state. Secondly, that according to which man has learnt to be more or less respectful of the personality of others in the context of existing laws, demanding of others the same respect towards himself and thus developing his own personality freely and spontaneously, undisturbed as to his individual requirements, or in voluntary collaboration with those who agree with him about collective requirements.

2) Let us for a moment attribute to these 'restorers' the maximum intelligence and good fortune in their prospective work. Let us suppose that they succeed everywhere, in the various states, in founding free institutions in which the sentiments of the traditional nationalities are respected in the best way possible; in which the sinister influences of particular groups are reduced to an insignificant level, so that the law really can rule equally for all; in which all protectionism and all restrictions on migration between countries are eliminated; in which all armaments expenditure is substantially reduced; in which, in short, the state directs its activity not at asserting supremacy abroad, but in pursuit of the common interests of its citizens.

In this case a revival, for a whole historical epoch, of national democratic civilisation would certainly be possible, purged indeed of the serious flaws that it had in the past. However it should be noted that, in all this scheme of things, the weakest point is that of international organisation. While in the national field the intelligent restorer understands that it is necessary not simply to trust to the good will of the citizens, but takes care to establish a solid body of laws provided with coercive power in order to contain and direct individual activities, the relations between the various states remain based exclusively on the peaceful goodwill of each of them, on the assumption that the interests of the individual states will coincide completely with the interest of the collectivity of the same states.

But this assumption is not true; on the contrary there is truth in the opposite assumption. In the absence of prohibitions, it is entirely possible to obtain an advantageous position that is damaging to others. In order for such an abuse to occur, it is not necessary to assume any particular perverse desire to subjugate; it is enough that a state thinks that its duty lies in procuring the well-being not of all mankind, but merely that of its own citizens.

The nation-state is constructed precisely for this aim; it is organically unsuited to seeing the interests of all mankind. A thousand and one occasions would present themselves at every moment, in which the interests of particular geographical groups are better favoured by damaging rather than respecting the interests of all the other countries. There would be nothing to hold one back from going down this road. But, once taken, it would be almost impossible to withdraw from the mechanism that obliges every state to defend injured interests from the abuses of others, ultimately resorting to force in order to uphold them. The progressive militarisation of individual countries would start once more, fatal to any healthy free regime. There would be a repeat of that cycle which has already been run twice, between 1870 and 1914 and between 1914 and 1938. National democratic restoration would therefore rest, even in the best of scenarios, on foundations as precarious as ever.

3) In reality however we have made the task of the restorers too easy, attributing to them intelligence and luck which no-one could reasonably expect. The reality within which the restorers must act is such that the slide towards militarism would become not only very probable, but even unavoidable. In the first place they are not suited to taking the necessary measures to create perfect national democracies. To proceed in this work they would need to know how to use, but not submit to, particular pressures coming from the grassroots. Instead, by their very nature, they are liable to adopt and express the spontaneous aspirations of the masses, to which they appeal as sovereign.

If we analyse the principal aspirations by which these masses are traditionally moved in the various European countries, we find that they are very susceptible to letting themselves be influenced by patriotic, class or sectional motives. This means that they are ready to demand from their leaders the defence or the realisation of interests concerning the power and the prestige of their country, or concerning the privileges of a particular class, or concerning the earnings of a particular market group. These interests may be well-founded or imaginary, but they are in any case always partial, and in effect absolutely regardless of the true general interest, however often they may be disguised as such.[64]

The democrats, wishing to represent the will of the people, would easily end up becoming, in their various tendencies, instruments of one particular group or another, aiming to win control of the state and to use its force to assert their particular interests. But any exclusive interest, economic, sentimental or ideological, wielding the unrestrained weapon of the sovereign state, would arouse analogous counter-measures from other states, rapidly poisoning the European atmosphere and generating new dangers of war.

Democratic mythology has a propensity to believe that wars are due only to the shady interests of small minorities and that the great masses are fundamentally peaceful. Therefore, it is thought, when governments are based on the latter, the danger of wars will be practically eliminated. It used to be said that wars were caused by the particular interests of absolute monarchs [65] and that war would disappear from the face of the earth on the day that in every country the peoples would have power to assert their peaceful intentions. Instead it has been seen that democracies, even those which most respected the rights of their citizens at home, by no means carried over this virtue into relations abroad, in which they remained selfish and inclined towards the exclusion and subjugation of rivals. In fact even in these democracies particularist interests were well able to assert themselves — sometimes those of the entire geographical group, at other times those of more restricted groups,[66] which ended up by pursuing the policy of absolute monarchs. The speed with which the new states emerging from the French and Russian Revolutions fully returned to the defensive and offensive foreign policy of their respective *anciens régimes*, barely disguising them with new words, may be instructive.

It is indeed not to be believed that there are strata of the population on whose aversion to war one can count as on a peculiar virtue. Pacifists are only the weak who know a priori that they are beaten, or that they will be used as instruments of the strong for ends that are not their own, and who deplore this state of affairs, as can well be understood. Those who can use force, if there is no superior law to impose discipline, are always inclined to use it to defend themselves, or to go on the offensive. Therefore a people, a class or any social group who are pacifist as long as they do not have access to power, will also be ready, when they hold it, to use it to obtain or defend a privilege. And in this attitude lies the root of bellicosity.

4) In the second place, such a restoration, centred on the sovereign nation-state, for this fact alone takes a fatal turn, even if we leave aside the democratic propensity to make itself spokesman of particularist interests felt by the masses.

When one speaks of the modern state, one must not only consider its ability to abuse its unlimited sovereignty. It is even more important to take account of the fact that around the state an entire, very powerful, historical tradition has been consolidated, which attributes to it a sort of absolute mystical value. The state has to obey unconditionally the categorical imperative which orders it to affirm and reinforce itself. Modern civilisation has succeeded in subduing feudal arrogance and quarrelsomeness only by transferring all the unlimitedness of rights from individuals to the sovereign state body which replaced them. It is interesting to note that precisely those countries whose regime has emerged from the feudal regime by direct descent have not gone through this phase of exaltation of the state; on the contrary, they have curbed it when it has tried to impose itself. These are therefore also the only countries which have not tried to attribute mystically to the state an absolute end in itself, always seeing it rather as purely an instrument for the realisation of common interests.[67] In all the other countries, more or less, and pre-eminently in seventeenth and eighteenth century France and in Germany in the nineteenth and twentieth centuries, the state has undergone this primitive deification, incarnated in the absolute monarchy. The European democracies have limited themselves to restricting its omnipotence in domestic affairs, leaving its transcendent absolute value intact in every other aspect; on the contrary, they have reinforced it with the addition of national passions which have increasingly developed as ever broader strata of the population began to participate in the life of the state, seeing their own fortunes linked to its destiny.

Now, it is certainly conceivable in the abstract that the democratic restorers might radically extirpate this tradition and reconstitute nation-states founded only on clear rational presuppositions, free from all mystical sovereign deification, (although if they were so free of the taboos of the sovereign state, it would be hard to understand why they should feel so urgent the need to reconstitute it despite its most evident drawbacks). But this radical reconstruction is in reality not possible, however little one reflects upon the real conditions which would face the restorers.

As has been said, they count on re-establishing popular freedoms, although they know that not everyone will be prepared to respect the rules of the game. So deeply rooted is their belief in the naturalness of the nineteenth century gentleman's code of conduct, so convinced are they that the masses are spontaneously capable of choosing the right way, that they believe ingenuously that they need only persuade people, for the veils to fall from eyes that wish only to see, and for the necessary majorities to be formed to make the democratic mechanisms function. But the fundamentally good man is a myth of the enlightenment; the masses (peoples, classes and others) in which a universal mission mystically resides are a romantic myth; and neither of the two myths stands up to critical examination. The masses, of whatever social class, are spontaneously capable only of protecting their own immediate interests, resorting to subjugation whenever they see the conditions for success. The citizen, able to respect the freedom of others and to cooperate freely with others, is perhaps the highest creation which the human spirit has succeeded in designing; but he is possible only on condition that there is a framework of institutions to discipline his impulses.

Therefore the democratic restorer can certainly dream of rose-tinted scenes of masses liberated from tyranny, which, while committing perhaps some accidental error or terrorist act in justified revenge, decide to exercise their sovereign right to proceed from the moment of liberation on the path of progress. However, as soon as he passes from dream to reality, he already has to start by relying on some solid traditionally recognised institutions, accepted by the people, which may constitute the first necessary legal framework within which civil liberties can be expressed.

The principal body available to fulfil this function is the nation-state. Far from radically destroying it, the restorer who wants to make a realistic policy must, at the critical moments, try to save all he can of the state's strength; he must hold up its pillars when they threaten to crumble, unless he wants to see his dream completely wrecked. Every other requirement takes second place to this one. That is the profound reason why German and Spanish democrats, to quote only the two most recent examples, proceeded with such caution with regard to the traditional institutions of their states, leaving intact the essential apparatus, despite their proclaimed aversion to them. And this is the profound motive for which in other countries the restorers are seen anxiously turning, when they feel the storm approach, to the most conservative institutions, for which they do not have any great sympathy but which they must hope remain standing, to provide them with solid support.

Now, a situation of this kind is really not the most propitious for ending the absolutist traditions which suffuse every pore of the European nation-state. These traditions may briefly be submerged by the popular tide, but will remain fixed in the way of thinking of the state bureaucracy, of the armed forces, of the magistracy and of the schools. Furthermore, they will seek to reaffirm themselves at every opportunity, gradually recovering lost ground as the first subversive wave subsides and people resume normal life, in which they once more see enthroned the divinity of the state. The history of the Weimar republic can be taken as the typical case of the problems in which the national democratic restorer finds himself inextricably entangled. In order to give Germany a democracy, the democrats had to conserve the mechanisms of order: bureaucracy, magistracy, military cadres. And these then swallowed up democracy.[68]

Finally we should not forget that, given the political importance the masses now have, a national democratic restoration would mean a series of broad measures towards greater economic equality. This means however that a greater number of constraints will be imposed by the activity of the centre on the activity of individuals and groups, i.e. a greater habit of discipline among the peoples. While therefore all the motives and occasions for international disagreements would remain, and while that same organisation to which Europeans traditionally attribute the uncontested right to call them to fight and to die would have been saved, social transformations would further develop to facilitate enormously the total and rapid militarisation of the various countries.

5) The absurdity of national democratic restorations is glaringly obvious if all the preceding considerations are applied to the concrete case of Germany, which constitutes the central problem of political life in Europe.* In Germany, its geographic position and historical traditions, the real or imaginary interests of different classes and of the entire people, the deification of state power, national arrogance, the existence of a landed aristocracy and of a vast class of officials accustomed to command, and the people's habits of obedience, would in an international system of sovereign states irresistibly impel any regime to make use of war. All these tendencies, even if they were momentarily repressed,

---

* *Editor's note.* Here again Spinelli's subsequent criticism of his Ventotene writing applies: American influence was decisive in the establishment of a solid German democracy. See p. 8 above.

would always remain very strong, even though in Germany a democracy was established, as happened in 1918; they would be even if one succeeded in breaking its state unity for a time, as some think of doing. The broadest concessions would not succeed in satisfying it, even if the politicians of other states were such fools as to show generosity, at the risk of soon seeing it armed and threatening, more formidable than before. The suspicions and restrictions which would foreseeably surround it would only help stiffen it in its aspiration to dominate. But with a Germany like this, no other country could afford not to be militarist.

After all these considerations one would have to be rather ingenuous to believe that with the restoration of national democratic states, there should be even the slightest likelihood of these setting out and remaining on the path of peaceful coexistence; and that after this they should arrive, in due course of time, at the necessary political maturity for all to be convinced of the appropriateness of a super-statal institution, so that federation would not be imposed on free peoples, but be merely the symbolic expression of the by now ingrained capacity to live without war. All that the sovereign states would be able to do in a moment of nausea at the horrors of war, would be a new League of Nations: an institution of only symbolic unity, devoid of any effective force, which would not remove a scrap of their sovereignty, and where the representatives of the powers would meet to make a show of their pacific intentions, until once more there was occasion to fight. And perhaps there would again be a series of conferences on disarmament, revolving around the insoluble problem of finding formulae in which each state should see the armaments of others reduced, without reducing their own.

It is hard to find another period in the history of mankind when civilised habits have been as widespread as in twentieth century Europe. The tragic agony of that period had few chance elements, and, almost as counter-evidence of its unavoidability, the same generation that saw the first catastrophe is now present at its repetition. Is there really nothing better to do than prepare oneself to run blindly for the third time through this cycle, accepting it as a fate from which one cannot extricate oneself? Then would not the racist solution be better, since despite the inevitable relapse into barbarianism, it would at least sweep away these absurdities?

Analysis of the restorationist tendency has thus brought us to the conclusion that, being the prisoner as much of the taboo of the sovereign nation-state as of that of popular sovereignty, it has become profoundly contradictory and is therefore quite incapable of inspiring the necessary activity and of freeing mankind from the errors in which it is floundering.

Communism and European unity

1) The culture of individuals and the civilisation of peoples are in direct proportion to how rich they are in effective goals and the extent to which they succeed in reconciling them. The progress of culture and civilisation therefore requires on the one hand the development of suitable instruments to attain certain goals, and on the other the harmonisation of different goals. The first task belongs to the intellect, which takes the goals as given, and which must aim only at logical rigour in forming its constructions. The second is the task of wisdom, which establishes the point beyond which it is no longer advantageous to pursue a particular goal, since otherwise others equally important would be suffocated by it; and seeks to concentrate attention on those which acquire a central value in relation to existing circumstances, and around which the others variously fall into order of importance.

Now, to be coherent, however difficult, is infinitely easier than to be wise. It frequently happens that the crystallisation of energies caused by the pursuit of a particular goal can so distort perspective as to hide its connection with other goals. And since the importance and usefulness of a goal depend precisely on this connection, the result of this rigidly deductive attitude is that even if that goal is reached, something deformed is accomplished, unworthy of the effort spent, and which does not contribute at all to the original intention of improving human life.

The most conspicuous deductive attitude of our times in the political field is that of communism, originally a response to the goals of the working classes to liberate themselves from the misery in which they find themselves and thus to have the opportunity to enjoy the fruits of civilisation from most of which they are excluded. It responds to a need therefore which falls naturally in the line of development of our civilisation. This is not the place to concern ourselves with the origin and development of communism as a whole, nor to ask ourselves whether the unilateral way it has determined or pursues its goal tends effectively to produce the desired broadening of modern civilisation. We are only interested in examining its position with regard to the problem of international anarchy.

It might seem that here we have finally stumbled across people who have got some idea of the solution. The communists have indeed long and vigorously denounced the imperialism which generates war, are not tied to nationalist taboos, and wish the union of the peoples. If however their propaganda is examined more closely, one perceives without any shadow of doubt that in reality the communists, like the democrats, have never seriously tackled the problem of international order, and hope that it will solve itself unaided. Although it is obvious that this problem has acquired a central importance, and that the significance of the other connected problems of our civilisation depend on how it is solved, yet the rigidly deductive communist approach fails to realise this and continues to believe that the central question is that of abolishing capitalism. Once this is achieved, all the rest would come about of its own accord, almost by divine grace. Socialist and communist internationalism is of the same type as that of the democrats. Just as the latter believe that the peoples will get along spontaneously once despotic regimes are eliminated, so the communists believe that the proletarians will abolish imperialism and war, purely as a result of abolishing capitalism in their countries.

Let us examine their attitude to our question more particularly.

After the period of the formulation of the so-called 'utopians' who thought of forming small autarkic communities, managed collectively, socialist thought widened its horizons and arrived at the idea that only a collectivist organisation embracing mankind as a whole could function effectively. This idea however was not a real directive for action, but constituted simply the imaginary projection into the future of tendencies which were assumed already to be operating irresistibly at that time. The socialists were convinced that the bourgeois regime was moving in this direction, and that there was nothing more to be done than carry on down that road. 'The delimitations and the antagonisms of the peoples,' wrote Marx in 1848, 'are in the process of disappearing, because of the very development of the bourgeoisie, because of freedom of commerce, because of the action of the world market, because of the uniformity of industrial production and because of the resulting conditions of existence. Those differences and antagonisms will disappear all the more because of the effect of the supremacy of the proletariat. Combined action, at least of the proletarians of civilised countries, is a prime condition for the liberation of the proletariat. To the extent that the exploitation of man by man will be abolished, so the exploitation of one nation by another will also be diminished. When the conflict between classes within the nation has gone, the antagonism between the nations themselves will also come to an end.'

As we see, the argument is as follows: a) existence of a bourgeois tendency to the elimination of international differences; b) abolition of class conflict within the individual nations; c) consequent automatic completion of the internationalist tendency. The combined action of the proletarians of the principal countries only has to follow a path already marked out. That no particular effort is needed to mark it out is demonstrated by the fact that although that concentration of action is considered as one of the prime conditions, nevertheless Marx did not feel any contradiction in the affirmation that immediately precedes the lines quoted: 'Since the proletarian of every country must before all else conquer political power, he must elevate himself to a national class and form a nation; therefore the proletariat is and remains national still, although in a sense quite different from that of the bourgeoisie'.

The Cobdenite view, which Marx fully accepted, according to which the intensification of trade between peoples would abolish national antagonisms, has turned out to be mistaken. It is true that grand capitalist interests favourable to free trade did and still do exist, but the actual development has been to reinforce national antagonisms, which have disturbed, slowed down and almost ended up by destroying trade. This contrast between theory and general historical development has brought the socialists, and thus the communists, to review their Cobdenite presupposition, but has not brought about any substantial alteration in the effective line of conduct of the proletarian movements.

It has in fact been gradually established, as Europe began to pile up armaments, that there was a different connection between capitalism and imperialism. This is not the place to criticise this theory, which generalises and gives the value of absolute law to particular cases of contingent significance, without analysing it in more detail.[69] We must however observe that compared to the major importance given in all the socialist literature to the danger of a war, and to the growing place which the internationalist theme took in its propaganda, there has been no effective action by the organised proletariat contributing to the creation of institutions capable of really reducing the danger of war, while there are acts which have contributed, even if involuntarily, to creating disagreements which accentuate international tension.

But the theory of capitalist imperialism was not meant to turn the efforts of the proletarians towards the struggle against war. It was a means of propaganda directed at attracting the anti-militarist forces onto anti-capitalist ground. On the one hand there was a realisation of the antithesis between military spending and social spending, and a consequent aim to reduce the former as much as possible; and on the other there was a more or less demagogic meeting halfway with an insubstantial pacifism, characteristic, as has been said, of those who feel themselves destined to be passive instruments and not active subjects of a bellicose policy.

2) In fact the effective proletarian policy continued, even after this theoretical correction, to remain a policy of national horizons, although the nation-states were becoming increasingly imperialist. This cannot be attributed simply to a chance instance of socialist myopia, and even less, as has sometimes been said, to their 'betrayal'. The restriction to the national context is linked to the effective direction of the parties aiming to establish collectivism. Every collectivist measure means in fact attributing the management of some economic sector to the supreme political power, i.e. to the power which men recognise as having the right to regulate their conduct.

In modern Europe, this supreme political power is that of the nation-state. This fact necessarily marked the limits of the nation. Strong dissension has always existed among socialists regarding the advantages of making the state take a gradually progressive series of collectivist measures, so as to give it a gradually more socialist character, or the advantages of a radical transformation in this direction to be reached by revolutionary means.

But these divergences, however important they may be from other points of view, are irrelevant to the question of the national or international character of the line to take. Leaving aside the socialist tendency (since it is much less coherent), let us examine the more consistent communist tendency. When prospects opened up during the last war for revolutionary action to establish a socialist order, the most rigorous politician of this tendency, Lenin, discussed the setting up of socialism as follows: 'The state appropriation of economic life, against which capitalist liberalism offers resistance, is by now an accomplished fact. Not only to free competition but also to the rule of trusts, of unions and of other economic monstrosities there is no sign of return. The question rests purely in the establishment of who in the future will be the regulator of state production: the imperialist state or the state of the victorious proletariat?' [70]

The socialist revolution was to be for him, in conformity with the marxist dialectic, the negation but also the most radical prosecution of the collectivism of war, which had already been to a greater or lesser extent realised by existing regimes. Lenin foresaw the realisation of the same process, at an accelerated rate and by means of a catastrophe, pursued by socialist reformers. As an instrument of socialist realisation, he could not therefore see any other than the existing nation-state, which had already started the work of collectivisation.

The communists declare however that, once they have eliminated the bourgeoisie which is guilty of conflict and war, the socialist nation-states would find no difficulty in unifying and planning the world economy in a unitary fashion.[71]

But this assertion is by no means proven. Indeed, all proof is precisely to the contrary.

In a collectivised economy, the state commands the principal resources of the country and proceeds according to plans. Therefore the necessary international exchanges and movements of workers could not happen spontaneously, but on the basis of treaties and agreements between the various socialist communities. We are faced not with a case of simple competition in which the terms of trade in goods and salaries are determined only by the market. On the contrary, the case of economic relations between socialist communities is of the type that economists have called competition between monopolies. Trade relations are indeterminate. Every richer and better-ordered community would tend to refuse to receive immigration from poorer countries, and particularly from those which were unable to establish a satisfactory political order. In a capitalist regime, international tensions usually come about because of restrictions placed on trade; in national socialist regimes tensions would come about whenever the need arose to make an exchange between communities. Economic disputes would be infinitely multiplied, transforming every foreign commercial relationship into a question of international policy, and generating hatred between countries rich in raw materials and countries poorly provided, between overpopulated countries and countries with a low demographic density.

And not only economic motives would generate friction. It may be supposed that communist states, springing from radical subversion, would find themselves, at least in principle, completely devoid of the mystical imperial spirit inherent in all the institutions of the modern state. But their basis would still be the nation, even though rid of the bourgeoisie, and the supreme task of the socialist state would remain that of providing for the interests of the inhabitants of the nation. The national differences with which for centuries the life of Europe has been interwoven, the disputes over the drawing of borders in zones with mixed populations, the need that every national community would feel to have an independent route to the sea etc., would not disappear because of the fact that the various national communities had become socialist.

To these traditional motives for friction would be added the new ideological dissensions which could arise among communist governments of various states, and which could no longer be settled with the ease with which the Third International now modifies the leaderships of communist parties. It is not easy to imagine a peaceful coexistence, for example between a state led by socialists and one led by communists, or between a Stalinist communist state and a Trotskyist one.

Closing this brief review of the international atmosphere in which the national socialist states would live, we have to say that the points around which irremediable conflicts could crystallise are innumerable, indeed they are multiplying; and the means to resolve them, non-existent. The conclusion to be drawn is easy to imagine: since responsibility for imperialism does not necessarily go back to capitalism, the abolition of the latter does not suppress imperialism but simply removes some sinister capitalist interests from the list of factors which feed it, adding by way of compensation some specifically socialist interests.[72]

3) One might object that Lenin's perspective indicates one way, but not the only possible way to achieve socialism; and that the communists, not being prisoners of any nationalist prejudice, could also put the struggle correctly in terms of international socialism and of international political power, corresponding more to their natural leanings towards internationalism. In reality it does not appear that there is the slightest attempt among them today to create such a position. Disorientated, like the democrats, by events which have overturned all their traditional schemes and which force them to fight alongside no less than the two most capitalist states in the world, they too now find refuge in the line of resistance of national democracy, hoping for the reconstitution of the sovereign democratic states. For them, as for the democrats, although for different motives, the nation-state is the necessary premise for the achievement of further goals. Strictly speaking, nothing should stop them, or some of them, from recognising that, since communism is realisable only on an international level, they need to prepare themselves to make plans to fight, if not for a single socialist world state which might be too difficult to build, at least for a European continental federation.[73] In actual fact, in order to move effectively onto the terrain of the federal struggle, the communists must apply rather a thorough self-criticism to their whole political way of thinking. This consists of a *Fixierung*, as Freud would say, of feelings, ideas, tactics, discipline and organisation around the question of the struggle against capitalism. Everything which does not come into these terms is subject to violent

deformation or is ignored. They are able to adapt mimetically to the strangest circumstances, but their point of reference is always the same. However, to see in capitalism the fundamental enemy to eliminate, implies proposing to transfer most of the means of production from private entrepreneurs to the state as soon as the chance arises. And the only existing state is the nation-state. This closes them in a magic circle.

In order to understand that the question of international order is much more completely bound up with problems of socio-economic order than they believe, that mind-set has to be broken. The central problem would become that of giving strength to the new international order, something that for the most part has nothing to do with the existence or otherwise of capitalism, but concerns the creation of political, judicial, administrative and military institutions. They should no longer appeal only to anti-capitalist feeling, since all the forces of free trade would be favourable to the new order. The problem of the collectivisations to be executed would still exist, but as one problem among others necessary for a more vital ordering of European society, and no longer as absolutely pre-eminent. Even if in a more distant future, when the sovereignty of the new federal state had become generally accepted as perfectly natural, as that of the nation-state is today, it should look again at the problem of whether to entrust to the federal state the exclusive management of the whole economy, it is certain that such a question could not be effectively proposed until after an entire epoch in which the fundamental political task had been that of consolidating the new, broader sovereignty. The fusion of the various national economies into a single European economy could not be seriously tackled by thinking of superimposing federal planning onto the various national collective systems, because this would presuppose an all-powerful federal government. Instead it would be necessary to give free rein to the spontaneous forces of commerce. That means it would be necessary to demolish most of the existing national collective systems, to one of which the communists feel themselves fundamentally tied, and, as for the others, they have always thought they need only push them a little further in the collectivist direction.

Would the communists be capable of executing such a revision of all their party line? Note that it is not a question of making a tactical manoeuvre. In our case that would be of very little use. In fact it is not a question of proselytising under a banner that serves to attract the ingenuous, in order then to proceed with the forces acquired to realise one's own programme of collectivisation to the extreme as soon as one has succeeded in seizing power. It is a question of understanding that precisely this programme is unsuited to the goal of European unity.

It is also worth indicating the implications of such a revision for the country where communism is already in power. To develop the theme of European unity in Russia means to make the Russian people take another step towards the sphere of European civilisation, and thus forms part of the centuries-old laborious Russian tendency to westernise itself. But it also involves dismantling much of the economic system created, and of the economic and political interests which have crystallised around it.

4) National collectivism is therefore not a remedy against imperialism. The subject is not exhausted, however, because it should still be borne in mind that the tendency to collectivism is not, as the communists believe, specifically proletarian. The proletariat, like all the poorest classes, has an interest in measures of collectivisation only to the extent that they are able to suppress privileges, monopolies, and in general avenues of exploitation for the exclusive advantage of individuals, which harm the collectivity. But, like any other non-parasitic class, the proletarians have an interest in being free to work and produce according to their choice and capacity and at their own risk.

The tendency to total collectivism is, on the other hand, profoundly inherent in the military state. A state whose most important goal is that of preparing for and waging war cannot help reaching out for all the human and material resources it needs. It is well known that Napoleon enacted many nationalising measures, and planned many more, not to respond to the interests of the bourgeoisie, but in order to gain control of greater resources to wage war. The only difference between Napoleonic times and our own is that now war no longer requires the use of only a portion of a country's wealth, but of practically one hundred per cent of the resources of a country where the state is sovereign; i.e. it is pushing towards the realisation of a radical collectivism. The examples of the last war and of this speak for themselves.

If we examine post-1918 history with an unprejudiced eye, we see that communism has indeed been victorious in only one country, but that there as much as in all the others where it has not succeeded or has been most severely repressed, nationalisation has made notable steps forward,[74] serving increasingly to facilitate and reinforce militarist policies. But this nationalisation has had little to do (except in the various common propaganda) with the effective emancipation of the working classes. Even in Russia, where it has been realised more than elsewhere following the communists' views, since they themselves have built socialism there, it has indeed contributed to bring forward a very backward people, but making them progress not so much towards an elevation of the working classes as towards greater military power. The loss of the freedom of movement for the workers and for the peasants, the growing differentiation between the tenor of life of the workers and that of the ruling bureaucracy, the severe repression of every freedom, leave many sceptical about the achievement of the first goal. The energy demonstrated in resisting Germany shows the achievement of the second.

The propagandist motives on which the communists depend to gather sufficient forces to make an assault on the capitalist citadel can be employed equally effectively to develop militarist collectivism, as the Nazis have most brilliantly demonstrated. The latter can moreover, in contrast to the communists, double the effectiveness of their propaganda by adding to anti-capitalist motifs those nationalist motifs which turn out to be the most profoundly felt by the common people today.

But even if, despite the formidable competition of the propaganda of militarist collectivism, the communists could succeed in gaining power in a whole series of countries and in establishing proletarian collectivism, they would have left absolutely intact the anarchic system of the nation-states with their 'sacred egoisms'; and they too would end up sliding inexorably into their adversary's terrain, militarist collectivism.

The European federation

1) It may be that our civilisation will not succeed in overcoming the present crisis, and that after long agony it will give way to more primitive and crude forms. There is no providential plan, no historical necessity which imposes its further continuation. If the latter should take place, it will only be because men will be able to concentrate sufficient attention and effort on identifying the evils undermining our civilisation and to put into effect the necessary remedies. And they will do this, if they are determined to preserve the main values of which it is composed. If no value is placed on freedom, i.e. on a type of society in which the individuals are not instruments of forces which transcend them, but autonomous centres of life; if no value is placed on justice, i.e. on a type of society in which freedom is not reserved for small privileged minorities, but is an effective and not only formal good, available to ever broader social strata: then it is not worth saving our civilisation. It is not possible to demonstrate that these goals *must* be pursued and we shall therefore not try to take on the impossible task. 'This subject', to use the words of

Meister Eckhart, 'is not addressed to anyone except those who feel it as much their own as their own life, or at least feel it as a heartfelt longing'.

But it is not enough to care about these values. One can care about them in an irrational way, unable to imagine their realisation other than in the old forms or in forms that follow in a unilateral and mechanical way. In both cases the result is, as we have seen, negative, because of the inability to perceive the reasonable coordination of goals and the suitable construction of means.

In the constantly varying harmony of the multifarious goals springing from European civilisation, from time to time some of them acquire a pre-eminent importance, setting the tone for all the others. Precisely because of the reciprocal relationship existing between all of them it is however not possible to go on to realise the central one completely every time, creating all the arrangements necessary to make it fully operative, and then pass gradually to the others. On the contrary, one's way of working can itself cause the order of importance to constantly shift, so that attention must be concentrated on another point. Thus, even before the completion of the civilising task of the absolute monarchies, extirpating feudal anarchy and establishing the rule of law within individual nations, it became more important to gradually involve larger and larger strata of the populations in determining laws themselves. And once the formation of a free political system was begun, the action against social inequalities was pushed to the fore. But this whole long and complex process sharpened the problem of international order, and now the possibility of harmoniously pursuing the other goals depends on how this is resolved. To believe that the evil arising from international anarchy will cure itself, and that things should continue to be taken care of according to the old order, is to have the politics of an ostrich. Left to itself, international anarchy turns into the destruction of modern civilisation, and into the constitution of a militarist empire based on the principle that the conquerors rule and the conquered become slaves. Failing to realise this is irrational, or, to use a simpler word, stupid.

If we wish to begin a rational examination of the problem of international order, we must start by answering these three main questions:

a) which rules are necessary to eliminate the present international anarchy?

b) are there forces in society sufficiently deeply interested in preserving these rules?

c) how can they be detached from the old traditions which have been revealed as inadequate and pernicious?

2) The evils of international anarchy do not derive from any causes extraneous to the absence of an international law, but precisely because of this absence. In order to provide for the common interest, there must be a suitable body capable of imposing the realisation of that interest. If that body is lacking, if the only institutions existing are suited purely to the achievement of particular interests, then, unless one believes in divine providence, it is clearly impossible to avoid a course of events in which each provides for his own particular interests, regardless of the damage inflicted on others and giving rise to conflicts and tensions which cannot be finally resolved except by resorting to force.

These evils cannot therefore be eliminated except by forming institutions to draw up and impose an international law which impedes the pursuit of goals advantageous only to one nation but damaging to others.

This solution appears self-evident, whenever it is a question of the internal order of a nation; but as soon as it is a question of international order, the people of our nationalistic age see it as strange, utopian and against human nature at its deepest and most immutable, and they strive to formulate sophisms to avoid facing it. The men of the feudal era once behaved in the same way regarding the formation of national units, since to them the only natural and obvious order appeared in the context of castles, counties and communes.

This international order can be created by means of an empire which reduces the other states to its vassals. The law then is that imposed by the dominant state; the necessary force to impose the law is that of the titular state of the empire. This is the most primitive method, and the most frequently realised in human history; and today we are witnessing an attempt to achieve it once more in the grand style, carried out with great coherence. If it is rejected, it is not because it uses violence to establish itself, but because for a whole era it would be based on violence, on the inequality of peoples, on exploitation by the dominator, on the mystical exaltation of the empire, on the further tendency towards universal domination, and on its permanently military character.

Yet this order can also be created in a way that conforms more to our fundamental requirements, through a federal organisation; this, while leaving each individual state the chance of developing its national life as best suits the degree and the peculiarities of its civilisation, removes from the sovereignty of all associated states the means by which they can assert their egoistic particularism, and creates and administers a body of international laws to which all must be equally subject.[75]

The powers which the federal authority must have at its disposal are those that guarantee the definitive end of exclusivist national policies. Therefore the federation must have the exclusive right to recruit and employ armed forces (which should also have the task of protecting internal public order); to conduct foreign policy; to determine the administrative boundaries of the various associated states, so as to satisfy basic national requirements and to make sure that there are no abuses of power over ethnic minorities; to provide for the total abolition of protectionist barriers and to stop them from being reinstated; to issue a single federal currency; to assure the full freedom of movement of all citizens within the boundaries of the federation; to administer all the colonies, i.e. all the territories still incapable of autonomous political life.

To carry out these tasks in the most effective way, the federation should have a federal judiciary; an administrative apparatus independent of those of single states; the right to raise the taxes necessary for its functioning directly from the citizens; bodies for legislation and control of the executive, based on the direct participation of the citizens and not on representation of the member states. This, foreshortened, is the organisation which could be called the United States of Europe, and which constitutes the indispensable condition for the elimination of imperialist militarism.

Given the pre-eminence which Europe still has in the world as a centre irradiating civilisation, and given that, with its internal struggles, it has always been the epicentre of all international conflicts, a definitive European pacification in the framework of federal institutions would mean the greatest advance towards world pacification that could be made under present circumstances.

3) Clearly it is not enough that a system has intrinsic merits. In order for it to be realised we have to see whether there are sizeable vital forces in modern civilisation which can be expected to side with it and support it permanently, forces that are not destined to dissolve rapidly, forces that feel they need that system in order to assert themselves and are therefore likely to act to uphold it. It would be useless to make a construction which no-one was interested in preserving, even if, owing to favourable circumstances, there were found sufficient forces to build it.

An investigation intended to identify these forces will not necessarily give us any indication as to what forces will be prepared to fight for the achievement of the federation. Many individuals and groups, however objectively interested in its realisation, could in reality find themselves so closely caught up in pursuing other orientations of feeling and action that they remain indifferent, ignorant and perhaps hostile to the path which would answer much better to their deepest interests. This will be the subject of further study in section 4. Here we wish only to see if the federation, should it succeed in being created, is to remain of interest only to a few political doctrinaires, or can instead really become a public good, felt as such by broad masses.

If we take a look at the field of European culture, we see that the moral education of large intellectual strata has been determined by currently predominating education systems. As regards intellectual considerations, they have a tendency towards nationalistic positions, as has been shown by the strong hold exerted in the field of middlebrow culture by chauvinistic and racist ideologies. But European culture has long overcome petty national boundaries, and its flowering is cosmopolitan. The highest state of European culture is beyond all nationalism; indeed, it is condemned rather to become sterile and perish if Europe proceeds any further on the nationalist path, since this course would remove the nourishment of free world-wide exchange of ideas and would hinder it from exercising its natural function of showing the less cultivated classes the paths to spiritual elevation. The European federation would guarantee intellectual cosmopolitanism and the possibility for high culture to exercise its function as guide. In this field, the federation could therefore count on the support of the highest and most fertile element, and on the resistance of broad groups of the most mediocre element; the latter would be destined to vanish when there was no longer a deliberate nationalistic policy interested in artificially forming spiritual attitudes no longer corresponding to the level actually reached by the spirit.

In the political field one must consider the hostility, which would certainly not cease with the establishment of federal unity, of those whose power is directly connected with the existence of the nation-states, and who would see their own power abolished or substantially lessened by the reduction of the latter's absolute sovereignty; by this we mean the present governing classes, the upper levels of the civil state apparatus, and even more the military. These constitute the most formidable obstacle, since they are the people with the greatest experience of command, and incarnate the strongest tradition of the European world. Even if thrown out of power, in the long run they would exert themselves to arrest, if not altogether destroy, the development of federal power. Behind them we find the parasitic, or in any case privileged strata of current society. In theory, they could maintain their situation as well in a federal system as in a nation-state. But since a European federation is not achievable except by a revolutionary crisis and using revolutionary forces,* i.e. merging its cause with that aimed at striking directly at all the privileged positions, these classes (consisting of the large-scale land-owners, leaders of companies to be nationalised, high ecclesiastical hierarchies, etc.) would certainly be induced to militate in the more congenial ranks of national reaction.

These hostile interests, which initially would be very strong when the loss of power was recent and therefore still rankled and the still vigorous nationalist idiocy was more easily exploitable, would not find nourishment in federal life however, and their trajectory would progressively decline. National sentiments, in their healthier aspects, would not necessarily be hostile. As it gradually became clear how a normal development of national requirements would be guaranteed much better by an impartial federal system, than by the various nations continually striving to dominate each other, national sentiments would come to lose their virulence and end up by coexisting peacefully in the federal context.

Among those interested in sustaining European unity on the other hand would be the progressive elements, as soon as they had realised what a fundamental guarantee it constituted for their effective functioning. The current development of militarism and national autarkies has directed an enormous quantity of resources towards unproductive war purposes. It has impeded more fruitful use of all energies and has pushed into aberrant ways, suffocated and paralysed those movements, especially those of the working classes, which could not resign themselves to accepting the existing social structure but aimed to modify it so as to satisfy their just demands. The European federation reduces to the minimum military expenditure, thus permitting the use of almost all

---

* *Editor's note*. Spinelli's criticisms of his Ventotene writing included its assumption that the federation would be rapidly established in a revolutionary crisis after the end of the war. Thus here and in the following pages he focused on such a situation and failed to consider how a federation might be established in more settled times. See p. 11 above.

resources for the purposes of raising the level of civilisation. With the abolition of absurd autarkic barriers it allows an immense development of production, thus creating the necessary conditions for a vital social transformation, i.e. based on a high standard of living. It causes the present necessity for permanent despotic regimes to disappear, leaving free play to movements for social emancipation.[76]

We can observe an analogous scene if we turn to the field of economic life. Here too we would find a strong initial difficulty, destined however to diminish with time, on the part of those who gain profits from national economic restrictions, on the part that is of the industrialists who profit from autarky, and of those classes of agricultural and industrial workers whose earnings are raised by various protectionist measures.[77] On the other hand, substantial support for unity will be found among those economic forces which are paralysed in their initiatives by national restrictions, i.e. those entrepreneurs who do not count on subsidies and protectionism to make their business profitable, but on the existence of large, rich markets,[78] and workers wishing to regain full freedom of movement, to go where they can to earn most by their work.

To conclude this rapid round-up, we may say that the European federation is not only a useful system in the abstract, but that in today's society there are sufficiently broad and solid forces and interests, which will increase even more in the future, to keep it alive and make it function effectively.

4) It now remains to examine the political aspect of the problem. The European federation may be the most rational solution of the present chaos. There may be, once it has emerged, very strong social groups interested in maintaining it. All this is clearly not enough. The most rational solution would not succeed in asserting itself if there were no forces to impose it. The strongest forces can remain ineffective if caught up in a mechanism which points them in quite another direction. Is it possible that an occasion might arise in which sufficient forces can be mobilised to impose this solution? If this question can be answered in the affirmative, it is clear that whoever cares about the fate of European civilisation should seriously set to work along these lines, whatever they might finally lead to for the fate of mankind. If on the other hand the answer should be negative, the entire preceding analysis will prove useless, and there will be nothing to do but resign oneself to a vain struggle yielding only poisoned fruits; one can draw aside in disdain, but with equally vain results.

In fact, the greatest difficulty inherent in the federal solution is not how to make it function effectively once it has emerged, but how to make it emerge. The idea of federation, except in the case of Switzerland, lies completely outside the European tradition. For many centuries the Europeans have followed the course of forming sovereign nation-states, and if there has sometimes been a glimpse of a chance to transcend this course, it has always been to return to the even more ancient Roman tradition; and one or other of the stronger nations has tried to build an empire, which is simply the final logical consequence of the national principle. The principal strength of the anti-federal interests is precisely this national tradition. We have already seen in the two preceding chapters how even the progressive forces have adapted to it, becoming entrapped by it, so that even the most recently formed traditions, democracy and socialism, accept the national terms of the political struggle and move within them, consigning to a dim and distant future, which does not commit them to anything, the task of overcoming the contradictions deriving from the principle of national sovereignties.

The obstacle lies in the force of inertia which pushes people to continue in the directions already taken. In order to achieve their interests, men develop laws, disciplines, habits, organisations, traditions. With the modification of the actual interests, however, these social and psychological mechanisms are not necessarily modified, their characteristic being rather their very permanence. Even when they have become harmful, they continue to be kept through the combined influence of those who are directly interested in maintaining them and those who, even though they do not or no longer have that interest, fail to see how else to proceed. The new and effective interests, not always having the force and the clarity of ideas necessary to clear away the old traditions, make compromises, adapt and often end up by creating disciplines and traditions which give a fatal and irrevocable turn to their efforts. The past does not only feed the present, but often suffocates and poisons it.

In support of particularist conservative interests and moral laziness, intellectual ingenuity then intervenes, exerting itself to demonstrate the absolute value of what exists merely because it exists. That which was the work of men, and can be unmade by men, is turned into something which leads them, whether they will or no. Innate qualities of leadership are discovered in the people launched on conquest. Or else it is affirmed that one cannot do violence to the profound aspirations of peoples and classes, but only realise what is in their consciousness. Necessary historical courses are identified; tradition weighs like a nightmare on living man and pushes him to proceed on a path which perhaps ends in an abyss, but which is the known, safe path traced by his forebears. '*Weh dir, daß du ein Enkel bist!*'

This profoundly reactionary line of argument, theorised at the beginning of the last century for explicitly reactionary motives, is to be heard blurted out at every step, in chorus, even if with various intentions. This is a proof not, as one deludes oneself, of 'sense of history', but of historical dullness, of the degree to which one is a prisoner, even though only unconsciously, of reactionary forces. Having a sense of history means understanding that 'the Sabbath was made for man and not man for the Sabbath'.

Reasoning according to romantic pseudo-historicism, we should certainly give a negative reply to our question: the European federation is unrealisable because none of the traditional ways which direct the great social forces and contribute decisively to influence the more striking forms of their consciousness moves in the direction of its realisation. Or, to use a fashionable term, the idea of the European federation is not a *myth* like that of the nation, democracy, or socialism.

Despite all that has been said up to now in favour of federation, the federalist idea would have no serious chance of translating itself into reality, if it was facing a world in a stable framework of traditional rules and organisations. Against their tremendous force of inertia, any force of reasoning, any propagandist ability, any ardour of passion would be condemned to be shattered. The same forces which should sustain it would remain trapped in the old schemes. European culture would continue to flower as best it could, remaining however quite incapable of breaking up the nationalistic pseudo-culture. The democratic forces would continue to attempt impossible compromises between free institutions and militarism; the socialist tendencies would continue to aspire to forms of socialism turning into militarist collectivisms. At the centre of all that, imposing as a divinity, there would remain the sovereign nation-state. The United States of Europe would continue to be a utopia, as they have always been until now.

In order that the United States of Europe should be achieved, there must be particularly favourable circumstances, in which the old traditions and old schemes of conduct, following very serious events, have temporarily lost their hold on individual minds; circumstances which offer the federalist tendency the opportunity to impose as a criterion for the fundamental division of minds, the attitude for and against European unity, and to assume the leadership of favourable forces, clearly indicating and confidently fulfilling the actions required to create the systems around which the interests indicated in the preceding pages can remain solidly united. And only then, by setting up new disciplines and raising new questions, would one come to create the new popular 'myth' of European unity. To wish this to exist beforehand would mean putting the cart before the horse.

Now these extraordinary circumstances are very likely to arise soon. All the most recent events are moving in this direction.

At the end of the last war, too, people felt the need to do something serious to avoid a repetition of the mistakes from which they had emerged. During the course of the war the need to carry out common actions had become apparent to the various states, actions which could have created embryonic superstatal political structures, such as joint command, common funds for the stability of exchange rates, distribution of available raw materials to maximise general productive efficiency, etc. In each camp, the most energetic states, i.e. England and Germany, had constituted the backbone of the entire coalitions of combatant states. And yet every country had in its spirit fought for itself, for its own defence, for the satisfaction of its own ambitions. In every country the common man watched what his own country did or left undone. The same characteristic of trench warfare taken from the struggle between the peoples made all attention concentrate on one's own frontiers. The years of war had subjected each state to hardship, but they had so to speak isolated it even more from all the others and from the vision of the common interest of the various peoples. Each one set out towards the post-war crisis closed within their national horizons. Within each state, the divisions created by problems of political organisation (democracy and authoritarianism) and those created by problems of property (socialism and capitalism) remained predominant. All these forces struggled bitterly to create an authoritarian or democratic, capitalist or socialist state, but always in order to increase the solidity of the sovereign state — the idol.

The proletarian movement which then occupied the foreground, and which could have exerted a decisive influence on international policy, was agitated and exalted by feelings of solidarity above all towards the Russian revolution. The Russian invitation to set up solid revolutionary parties, capable of achieving a world revolution, was not however accepted by the vast majority of workers. They showed by their deeds that they sympathised with the Russian revolution but wanted to pursue their traditional policy in national terms. Thus in the field of international policy, almost the only effect of the Russian myth was to raise hopes that the past could be restored, leaving completely in the shade throughout the critical post-war period the question of organising peace in the world, and in particular on the European continent. Although this was effectively the crucial thing as regarded the future development of mankind, it remained entrusted to elder statesmen who, it could almost be said because of professional bias, were not capable of seeing beyond the problems of national power, and who sought to obtain, according to their abilities and the forces which they had behind them, within the limits of peace which succeeded those of war, one advantage or another. Only a very few understood the danger of reconstituting the absolute sovereignty of the European states.[79] This being the state of affairs, it is easy to understand how the need to set up an international order should have produced only the abortive League of Nations.[80]

The present war has followed a totally different course. Excluding England, half of Russia and some secondary western states, the entire continent finds itself, for the most part directly and to a lesser extent indirectly, under the domination of Germany. The old state structures are shattered or remain standing only in appearance. This state of affairs, which in the case of a German victory would constitute the point of departure for the German empire, would, if the contrary should happen, constitute the most favourable situation for the affirmation of the federalist idea. The present German domination in fact impels the various peoples to free themselves, but sets this need not as a particular need of each people, but as the common interest of all the European peoples. Even now popular feelings are losing their national narrow-mindedness; increasingly the peoples are following with their hearts, not the fate of their own flag, but the fates of the forces that fight for them, even if officially they are the forces of an enemy country. All the countries are beginning to realise that the problem for which they are fighting is a problem superior to that of the power of their own nation. If the military power of Nazism is shattered, all the European countries would find themselves simultaneously facing the problem of giving an ordered system to the continent. The depth of suffering borne and of the danger of general enslavement would make this necessity urgently felt. The problem of international order would be superior to that of national order, to an extent that at the end of the last war was certainly not felt. The sovereign nation-states would not be there before us, solid and powerful, to attract the attention of all. On the contrary, the tragic impotence of these idols would be profoundly imprinted on the mind of all, of the defeated, the victors and the liberated. The reactionary nationalistic tendencies, disguising themselves according to the passions of the moment, could seek once more to yoke to their cause the national passions offended by the recent oppression, but they could not simply monopolise them at will. A federalist political movement could spoil their game by also addressing itself to these same passions and seeking to guide them towards a solution which does not ignore national sentiments, but rather gives them the way to manifest themselves freely. Given the freshness of the memory of war, the tone of the moment will not be that of an aggressive nationalism, but will be the desire no longer to see one's own nation oppressed, and to find a way of living in peace with one's neighbours. The federal solution would meet these aspirations much better than the simple restoration of national sovereignties. It would certainly be a hard struggle, requiring energy and skill to reach the goal. If it were a question of creating a unitary state, national sentiments would be united against it, and it would be difficult to mobilise sufficient forces to overcome it. But for a federal solution it would not be necessary to divide national passions, but rather to use them as a broad source of support, preventing the link between them and the forces of nationalism from being re-established. Finally it should be remembered that, given the development of events, it is foreseeable that the definitive crisis will not come in isolated fashion, first in one country and then in another, but all over Europe at once, at the moment of the collapse of the military power which now holds almost all of it in thrall. This will enormously facilitate the coordination of propaganda and action in all the countries.

The federalist idea, being thus placed on the agenda as aiming to resolve the most urgent of all post-war problems, and directly affecting the nation-state, the body towards which all the traditional movements that mobilise the masses are oriented, could not but have a profound effect of reform and clarification on democratic and socialist aspirations. These tendencies too would not present themselves, as they did at the end of the last war, with trained political cadres and organised masses accustomed to following their directives, in a word, with the force of a consolidated tradition.

While there will be an enormous desire for freedom, ideas on how to achieve it will be highly uncertain. The memory of the corruption which is concealed in the national democracies, condemned to be a hopeless alliance between democracy and militarism, will be very vivid in everyone's minds. We can already see how this memory makes all the democratic countries confused and uncertain. The federalist movement would have to gather together the living forces in this field too. It would have to penetrate into the midst of the powerful but disorganised masses, showing the one way possible to realise that aspiration permanently, and thus stopping them from falling back into the power of traditional national democratic ways. Here too it is not a question of ignoring and fighting the need for liberty which is stirring in the hearts of peoples, weary as they are of totalitarian despotisms. It is not a question of going in search of other forces to oppose this, but of knowing how to direct existing aspirations.

And if, finally, the socialist tendencies of the working classes are taken into consideration, it can be seen that they are very far from being satisfied, and that in the post-war crisis they will make themselves urgently felt. But it is no longer a question of passions already set and directed towards precise goals. On the contrary. The old proletarian parties have been deprived of their traditional organisational hold on the masses, and experience in the period from 1918 until today has confused all their ideas, making them highly uncertain as to the future path to follow. Suffice it to compare, to take only the case of the most energetic among them, the confident boldness with which the socialists of revolutionary tendency (i.e. those who were very soon to become communists) declared during the last war that soon the time would come for the establishment of socialism, and the caution with which the communists express themselves today, often using generic democratic terms. This is due partly to clever tactics, and, since they have not modified anything in their fundamental conceptions, it would be hard to understand precisely why they should not follow the very same road of ultra collectivisation followed by Russia, as soon as the opportunity offered. But that they have felt the need to leave their visions in shadow is a notable symptom of how they themselves no longer feel collectivisation corresponds to their socialist proletarian aspirations. National collectivisation (and in practical terms, as has been seen, no collectivisation is possible today except on a national scale) no longer has the charm of the unknown. At the end of the war, the socialist aspirations of the proletariat will not be met by the old schemes either. The federalist movement will be able to work effectively to direct them favourably towards a European solution, advocating radical reforms and showing how they can really bear fruit only in an environment freed from the imperialist nightmare.

Each country will have its particular problems to solve. To solve them all in a homogeneous and unitary manner, to coordinate all the highly disparate movements, would be a hopeless undertaking. But the federalists should not attempt to do this, since they do not intend to create a unitary European state. The federalist idea, profoundly innovative as it may be, is so elastic as to be able, in a revolutionary situation, quickly to become the distinguishing criterion of political forces and existing passions, not opposing itself to them, but imbuing them with itself and rendering them thus immune to the fatal deficiencies of the old orientations. It will be enough if it can, by proceeding intelligently, show these profoundly disorientated national, democratic and socialist forces and passions that the essential condition for the adequate resolution of their demands is the formation of the few, simple, easily comprehensible, solid and irrevocable federal institutions. It will not be necessary to worry too much about the coordination of individual national problems. The creation of the federation would in fact involve the creation of the internal order to which the progressive forces would naturally coordinate themselves and which would leave its imprint on them from then on.

5) From what has been said, it seems clear that the greatest difficulty to overcome in order to succeed is not the existence of old traditions, since these will be broken and dispersed, or at least uncertain and disorganised. The major difficulty is in the formation of the federalist movement. Without it the extraordinary conjunction of favourable conditions would melt away without being exploited. What is required of active federalists is much more than what is required of the masses that can be mobilised in favour of European unity. Yes, they have to understand the value of the demand for national independence, political liberty and social equality, but they must also immunise themselves, by means of serious self-criticism, against all the national, democratic, socialist fetishes, i.e. the traditional, inadequate ways with which until now people have tried to satisfy these requirements. If they have this immunity they will be capable of exerting influence on the masses and guiding them towards objectives to which they have already been unconsciously predisposed by all the historic events.

If instead they are prisoners of the various current fetishes and symbols, they will be quite incapable of fulfilling that function of leadership. They will not have the open-mindedness and firmness necessary to hold the multifarious forces together and to restrain them when in their one-sidedness they threaten to put paid to the goal; they will not be capable of giving order to the chaos of the masses, but will be swallowed up by it.

finis

Further Reading

Those who would wish to read British publications relevant to European federalist thought from the mid 1930s to the early 1960s are recommended the following:

Federal Union pamphlets, including:

Federal Union and the League of Nations, Richard Law MP, 1939

Federal Union, foreword by Sir William Beveridge, 1940

Federate or Perish, 1940

War Aims, 1940

'Federation: Peace Aim - War Weapon', *Federal Union News*, no. 88, June 1942

Federal Union Official Policy, 1942

Federation: Target for Tomorrow!, 1942

Exploring Tomorrow, Charles Kimber, 1943 or 1944

Federation: Target for Today!, 1944

Europe: The Key to Peace, F.L. Josephy, 1944

Questions and Answers on Federal Union, 1946

Draft of a Federal Pact, 1949

Let the Argument Proceed, 1950

Federal Union 21, 1959

Federal Union, 1962

Federal Union Twenty-Five, 1964

Beveridge, Sir William, *Peace by Federation?* (Federal Union, 1940), reprinted in Royal Institute of International Affairs, *World Order Papers,* First Series (London: RIIA, 1940).

Beveridge, Sir William, *The Price of Peace* (London: Pilot Press, 1945).Beveridge, Lord, *For World Government* (London: Crusade for World Government, 1948).

Brugmans, Dr H., *Fundamentals of European Federalism* (Federal Union, 1947).

Catlin, George, *One Anglo-American Nation: The Foundations of Anglosaxony as a Nucleus of World Federation: A British Response to Streit* (London: Andrew Dakers, 1941).

Chaning-Pearce, M. (ed.), *Federal Union: A Symposium* (London: Jonathan Cape, 1940), contributors include Sir John Boyd Orr, W.B. Curry, L.W. Grensted, Ivor Jennings, G.W. Keeton, R. J. Mackay, J. Middleton Murry, J.B. Priestley, Patrick Ransome, Lionel Robbins, Georg Schwarzenberger, Olaf Stapledon, H. Wickham Steed, Duncan Wilson.

Curry, W.B., *The Case for Federal Union* (Harmondsworth: Penguin Special, 1939).

Curtis, Lionel, *Civitas Dei* (London: Allen & Unwin, 3 vols, 1934-7), reprinted in 1938 in one volume as *The Commonwealth of God,* and again as *Civitas Dei,* in a revised edition, in 1950.

Curtis, Lionel, *The Way to Peace* (London: Oxford University Press, 1944).

Curtis, Lionel, *World War: Its Cause and Cure* (London: Oxford University Press, 1945).

Curtis, Lionel, *World Revolution in the Cause of Peace* (Oxford: Blackwell, 1949).

Curtis, Lionel, *The Open Road to Freedom* (Oxford: Blackwell, 1950).

Davies, Lord, *A Federated Europe* (London: Gollancz, 1940).

de Rougement, Denis, *The Way of Federalism: Totalitarianism and Federalism* (Federal Union pamphlet, undated, 1949?).

Greaves, H.R., *Federal Union in Practice* (London: Allen & Unwin, 1940).

Hart, Norman (ed.), *Basis of Federalism: A Symposium*, with contributions by Alexandre Marc, Sir John Boyd Orr, Abbé Groues Pierre and Henry Usborne MP (Paris: World Student Federalists, 1949).

Jennings, W. Ivor, *A Federation for Western Europe* (Cambridge: Cambridge University Press, 1940).

Kimber, Charles, *Exploring Tomorrow* (Federal Union booklet, 1943 or 1944), with contributions from Bentwich, Joad, Josephy, Keeton, Kimber, Liddell Hart.

Kitzinger, Uwe, *The Challenge of the Common Market* (Oxford: Blackwell, 1961).

Lambert, John and Michael Shanks, *Britain and the New Europe:The Future of the Common Market* (London: Chatto & Windus, 1962).

Lothian, Lord (Philip Kerr), *Pacifism is not Enough (nor Patriotism Either)* (London: Oxford University Press, 1935), reprinted with a preface by Sir William Beveridge (1941).

Mackay, R.W.G., *Federal Europe* (Michael Joseph, 1940), revised and republished as *Peace Aims and the New Order* (London and New York: Michael Joseph, 1941).

Mackay, R.W.G., *Britain in Wonderland* (London: Gollancz, 1948).

Mackay, R.W.G., *Western Union in Crisis: Economic Anarchy or Political Union* (Oxford: Blackwell, 1949).

Mackay, R.W.G., *The Economic Aspects of European Federation* (Oxford: Blackwell for Federal Trust, 1952).

Mackay, R.W.G., *Whither Britain?* (Oxford: Blackwell for Federal Trust 1953).

Mackay, R.W.G., *Towards a United States of Europe* (London: Hutchinson, 1961).

Mayne, Richard, *The Community of Europe* (London: Gollancz, 1962).

Pinder, John, *Britain and the Common Market* (London: Cresset Press, 1961).

Pinder, John, *Europe Against de Gaulle* (London: Pall Mall Press for Federal Trust, 1963).

Pryce, Roy, *The Political Future of the European Community* (London: John Marshbank for Federal Trust, 1962).

Ransome, Patrick (ed.), *Studies in Federal Planning* (London: Macmillan, 1943), with chapters by Lord Lothian, K.C. Wheare, C.E.M. Joad, Lionel Robbins, Norman Bentwich, Lord Lugard, Gilbert Walker, H.R.C. Greaves, A.L. Goodhart, Barbara Wootton, George Catlin, K. Zilliacus.

Robbins, Lionel, *Economic Planning and International Order* (London: Macmillan, 1937).

Robbins, Lionel, *The Economic Causes of War* (London: Jonathan Cape, 1939), reprinted, with a new preface (New York: Fertig, 1968).

Russell, Bertrand, *Which Way to Peace?* (London: Michael Joseph, 1936).

Streit, Clarence K., *Union Now: A Proposal for a Federal Union of the Democracies of the North Atlantic* (London and New York: Jonathan Cape and Harper, 1939); first chapter reprinted as *America Speaks* (London: Federal Union pamphlet, 1939).

Usborne, Henry, *Towards World Government: The Role of Britain, Peace Aims* (London: National Peace Council Pamphlet, 1946).

F.A. Hayek, *Individualism and Economic Order* (London: Routledge & Kegan Paul, 1949) pp. 255-72.

Wheare, K.C., *Federal Government* (London: Oxford University Press, 1946).

Wickham Steed, H., *Our War Aims* (London: Secker & Warburg, 1939).

Wilson, Duncan and Elizabeth, *Federation and World Order* (London: T. Nelson & Sons, 1939).

Retrospectively, Patrick Ransome's *Studies in Federal Planning* has been reissued by the Lothian Foundation Press, with an introduction by Sir Charles Kimber, in 1990. This is available from the Federal Trust.

Other important publications are:

Lipgens, Walter, *A History of European Integration 1945-1947: The Formation of the European Unity Movement* (Oxford: Clarendon Press, 1982).

Lipgens, Walter (ed.), *Documents on the History of European Integration: Vol. 1, Continental Plans for European Union 1939-1945; Vol. 2. Plans for European Union in Great Britain and in Exile 1939-1945* (Berlin and New York: de Gruyter, 1985, 1986).

Pinder, John and Bosco, Andrea, *Pacifism is not enough: Collected Lectures and Speeches of Lord Lothian (Philip Kerr)*, with a foreword by the Hon. David Astor (London & New York: Lothian Foundation Press, 1990). This is available from the Federal Trust.

Notes

[1] Altiero Spinelli, *Come ho tentato di diventare saggio: vol.1, Io, Ulisse* (Bologna: Il Mulino, 1984), p. 145.

[2] Ibid., p. 253.

[3] Riccardo Faucci, *Einaudi* (Torino: UTET, 1986), p. 223.

[4] Altiero Spinelli, *Io, Ulisse*, pp. 302, 306, and *Come ho tentato di diventare saggio: vol.2, la goccia e la roccia*, posthumously edited by Edmondo Paolini (Bologna; Il Mulino, 1987), p. 40.

[5] *Io, Ulisse*, p. 301.

[6] Luigi Einaudi, *Lettere Politiche* (Bari: Laterza, 1920). The articles were again reprinted in his *La guerra e l'unità europea* (Bologna: Il Mulino, 1986).

[7] The Federal Union Research Institute was the forerunner of the Federal Trust; see John Pinder, *European Unity and World Order: Federal Trust 1945-1995* (London: Federal Trust, 1995).

[8] Giovanni Agnelli and Attilio Cabiati, *Federazione Europea o Lega delle Nazioni?* (Torino: Bocca, 1918), reprinted in the 1970s with an introduction by Sergio Pistone (Torino: Edizione E.T.L, 1979). For a survey of federalist writers in the British liberal tradition, see John Pinder, 'The federal idea and the British liberal tradition', in Andrea Bosco (ed.), *The Federal Idea, vol.1: The History of Federalism from the Enlightenment to 1945* (London: Lothian Foundation Press, 1991).

[9] Lionel Robbins, *Economic Planning and International Order* (London: Macmillan, 1937), and *The Economic Causes of War* (London: Jonathan Cape, 1939). It was Spinelli's translation of the latter that was published as Lionel Robbins, *Le cause economiche della guerra* (Torino: Einaudi, 1944). One of Spinelli's essays was 'Gli Stati Uniti d'Europa e le varie tendenze politiche', reproduced below as 'The United States of Europe and the Various Political Tendencies', and the other was 'Politica marxista e politica federalista', both published originally in 1944 in Rome by the Movimento Italiano per la Federazione Europea, as A.S. e E.R., *Problemi della Federazione Europea*, and reprinted in Spinelli - Rossi, *Il Manifesto di Ventotene* (Napoli: Guida editori, 1982).

[10] Interview with Altiero Spinelli by Sonia Schmidt, English translation in Altiero Spinelli - Ernesto Rossi, *The Ventotene Manifesto* (Ventotene: The Altiero Spinelli Institute for Federalist Studies, 1988), pp. 50-66. Beveridge's text will have been his Federal Tract No.1, *Peace by Federation?*, reproduced below. Wootton's was most likely *Socialism and Federation*, Federal Tract No.6 (London: Macmillan, 1941). Layton's was probably his pamphlet *The British Commonwealth and World Order* (London: News Chronicle by arrangement with the Oxford University Press, 1944).

[11] *Io, Ulisse*, pp. 307-8.

[12] Wilson was also listed in Beveridge's Federal Tract as the author of a forthcoming Tract entitled 'Federalism under Discussion', which was, however, never written because Wilson went soon afterwards to serve in the wartime Civil Service.

[13] *Economic Planning and International Order*, p. 239, and p. 56 below.

[14] See F.A. Hayek, 'Economic Conditions of Inter-State Federalism', *New Commonwealth Review*, Vol. 5, No. 2, September 1939; reprinted in F.A. Hayek, *Individualism and Economic Order* (London: Routledge and Kegan Paul, 1949), pp. 269-70. Einaudi sent one of Hayek's books to Rossi, which Spinelli cites in his essay on 'The United States of Europe ...' (see note 76 below).

[15] 'Politica marxista e politica federalista', in *Il Manifesto di Ventotene*, pp. 94-148.

[16] pp. 88-90 below.

[17] 'Politica marxista e politica federalista', pp. 113-4, 137.

[18] Loc. cit.; and 'The United States of Europe', below p. 104.

[19] See *Io, Ulisse*, pp. 257-8. Apart from the enunciation of fundamental democratic principles, the Manifesto dealt with the defects of fascism rather than the strengths of liberal democracy; and the section on democracy and European unity in the essay on 'The United States of Europe ...' (pp. 90-97 below) does not take account of the situation of mature democracies.

[20] See 'The United States of Europe ...', p. 98 and note 67 below.

[21] Ibid., p. 99.

[22] *Io, Ulisse*, pp. 311-12.

[23] The Ventotene Manifesto, pp. 80, 82 below.

[24] pp. 108-09 below.

[25] 'The Ventotene Manifesto', p. 82, 'The United States of Europe ...', p. 109, below.

[26] 'The United States of Europe ...', p. 110 below.

[27] Ventotene Manifesto, p. 81 below.

[28] 'Politica marxista e politica federalista', p. 142.

[29] Extracts from this section are given in pp. 82-3 below. It is printed in full in *The Ventotene Manifesto* (Altiero Spinelli Institute edition), pp. 34-8.

[30] *Io, Ulisse*, p. 311.

[31] Ibid., p. 317.

[32] 'Politica marxista e politica federalista', p. 138.

[33] See 'The United States of Europe ...', p. 119 below.

[34] *Io, Ulisse*, p. 312.

[35] *The Ventotene Manifesto* (Altiero Spinelli Institute edition), p. 39.

[36] Richard Mayne and John Pinder, with John Roberts, *Federal Union: The Pioneers - A History of Federal Union* (Basingstoke: Macmillan, 1990), pp. 26-7; the citation is from a statement by Archbishop William Temple.

[37] Ibid., p. 100, and John Pinder, 'Speak Truth to Power: The British Federalists and the Establishment', translated into Italian in Sergio Pistone (ed.), *I movimenti per l'unità europea dal 1945 al 1954* (Milano: Jaca Book, 1992), pp. 125-6.

[38] R.W.G. Mackay, *Towards a United States of Europe: An Analysis of Britain's Role in European Union* (London: Hutchinson for the Federal Trust, 1961).

[39] See Sergio Pistone, 'Il ruolo di Altiero Spinelli nella genesi dell'Art. 38 della Comunità Europea di Difesa e del progetto di Comunità Politica Europea', in G. Trausch (ed.), *La construction de l'Europe, du Plan Schuman aux Traités de Rome: Projects et initiatives, déboires et échecs* (Brussels: Bruylant, 1992).

[40] See Jean Monnet, *Les Etats-Unis d'Europe ont commencé: Discours et allocutions 1952-1954* (Paris: Robert Laffont, 1955), pp. 55-60.

[41] See Altiero Spinelli, *Diario europeo 1948/1969*, edited by Edmondo Paolini (Bologna: Il Mulino, 1989), pp. 140, 142-5.

[42] Conversation with Spinelli at that time.

[43] Richard Balfe and Brian Key, Labour, and Stanley Johnson, Conservative. Of the other five who responded, three were Italian and two German.

[44] Derek Prag MEP, 'A New Framework?', *Facts*, Sept./Oct. 1982, p. 6.

[45] 'Report of the Ad Hoc Committee on Institutional Affairs to the meeting of the European Council in Brussels on 29 and 30 March 1985' (Dooge Report), *Bulletin of the European Communities* 3/1985.

[46] *The Truth about the Peace Treaties*, vol. i, p. 404.

[47] *Populaire*, Oct. 14 and 10, 1939.

[48] 29 December 1939, in a speech to Senate.

[49] For these quotations from speeches by Lord Cecil (in 1919 and 1920) I am indebted to Professor E. H. Carr's recent volume *The Twenty Years' Criss*. It should be added that these quotations by no means represent the whole of Lord Cecil's attitude. He has been a consistent advocate of further sanctions when needed.

[50] Mr Winston Churchill in *Step by Step*, p. 38.

[51] *The Twenty Years' Crisis*, pp. 137, 139.

[52] It was also published as a chapter in Patrick Ransome (ed.), *Studies in Federal Planning* (London: Macmillan, 1943), available from the Federal Trust.

[53] It would be out of place in this context to elaborate the details of a desirable framework. The main preoccupation of this work is with the broadest outline of different types of plan considered in their international aspects. But it is perhaps permissible to say here that, in the opinion of the author, it is in the discovery of improvements in the admittedly defective framework of the present that one of the most important paths of future reform consists. It is not *certain* that on every possible occasion the mechanism of markets will function satisfactorily. But experience suggests that in most cases where it does not investigation shows that there is some deficiency in the law. These deficiencies are often apparently trifling. To discover them is a dull matter involving hard work and little emotional satisfaction. But it is difficult to exaggerate the practical significance of such studies. It is only necessary to compare the radically different evolution of industrial structure in England and in Germany to realise how important apparently unimportant differences in the law may be. It may be suggested that if half the energy which has been put into discovering ways in which the monopolistic activities of private enterprise may be superseded by the monopolistic activities of government organs had been devoted to discovering ways of preventing private enterprise acquiring legalised monopolistic power, the so-called monopoly problem would have ceased to be very important.

[54] Adam Smith, *The Wealth of Nations* (Cannan's Edition), vol. II, pp. 184-185, where an excellent short discussion of the functions of governments in this respect is to be found.

[55] Ibid. p. 435.

[56] This is a subject which Cannan made his own long before it was a matter of popular discussion. See especially his valedictory address to the London School of Economics, 'Adam Smith as an Economist', *An Economist's Protest*, p. 41 seq. Also a lecture on 'International Anarchy from the Economic Point of View', reprinted in the same place, p. 65 seq.

[57] Hamilton, *The Federalist* (Everyman Edition), p. 20.

[58] Ibid. pp. 71, 72.

[59] I cannot help thinking that my friend, Mr E. L. Woodward, makes just the wrong point against Cobdenism when (in his interesting essay on *War and Peace in Europe* 1815-1870) he asks would such thinkers have been willing to 'apply, as between state and state, forms of cooperation and mutual aid which they rejected in a sphere more directly under their control'? (p. 71). So far as the sphere directly under the control of the national states was concerned, no Cobdenite ever thought of rejecting the coordinating aid of the framework of law and order. If they had been willing to see established, between state and state, the form of organisation which they supported within states, the international anarchy would have disappeared. Support of a policy of permitting, within a coordinating framework of law, the free movement of capital and labour, is not support of a policy permitting sovereign individuals to do exactly as they please; and there would have been no inconsistency in demanding an apparatus of international co-ordination and coercion while holding that within such a framework the common interest might best be served by a system of decentralised initiative resting on private property and the market.

[60] For a good account of these see Raymond Buell, *Death by Tariff*, Chicago University Press.

[61] See e.g. Dr E. R. Glover's *Pacifism and Sadism* - a good example of the way in which one of the profoundest discoveries of our age can be made ridiculous by superficial application. In is interesting to compare Dr Glover's wearying épatism with the restraint and insight of Freud. See especially *Civilization, War and Death*, passim.

[62] For a fuller elaboration of these arguments see my *Economic Planning and International Order*, chaps. ix, x and xi. The general argument of Mr Clarence Streit's *Union Now* should also be consulted.

[63] Perhaps a word is necessary here concerning the relation of the suggestion here put forward and that put forward by Mr C. K. Streit. Mr Streit's scheme, it will be remembered, is for a union of the Atlantic democracies including the United States and the British Empire. I have no objection to this. If Mr Streit could induce his fellow-countrymen to come forward with the proposal, I should be delighted to see our government accept it; the larger the federation, the smaller the area of future war. But I think it very unlikely that this will happen, It does not seem probable that in our generation at least, the citizens of the United States will feel that compelling urge to union with other peoples which would alone make it possible. On the other hand, the disunity of Europe is so great and the evils likely to result from its persistence are so frightful, that it seems possible that, out of the extremity of our danger, a movement for unity might arise. After all there is a common European consciousness; and it is surely in the logic of history that sooner or later this should be enshrined in common political institutions. I see no insurmountable difficulty in the relation of the British Dominions to a federal Europe. Either they could enter the federation as full members; or they could retain via the British Crown the same loose relation as exists at present. I see much greater difficulty in the inclusion of Russia. For Russia is not European in spirit; and totalitarian dictatorship is incompatible with the federation of free peoples.

[64] Patriotic motives, i.e. precisely those which are most easily converted into national vainglory and a propensity to oppress other peoples, are the most strongly felt in the modern age. Suffice it to recall one of the most striking cases: on 14 January 1935, the inhabitants of the Saar were called on to decide if their country should remain under the administration of the League of Nations for another ten years, or return to Germany, or come under France. The inhabitants of the Saar were almost entirely organised workers, fond of their freedom, and for the most part Catholic. They had been informed in detail, by a very lively anti-Nazi campaign run among them by numerous German political exiles, as to what an immediate return to Germany would mean under Hitler's government. A corps of Anglo-Italo-Dutch-Swedish troops ensured order, guaranteeing a secret ballot. The plebiscite showed 476,089 votes for Germany, 46,613 for the status quo and 2,083 for France. Nationalistic feeling was so overwhelming that those same workers did not even seriously consider the option of delay, which would have compromised nothing, and declared themselves by a spectacular majority for immediate unity with the *Reich*, i.e. for the destruction of their trade union organisations, for the persecution of their religion, and for the loss of their freedom.

[65] The current translation of this democratic manichaeism is the assertion that wars are caused, if not by the greed of the prince, by the greed of the capitalist oligarchy. The reply given here to such an argument is therefore valid for this theory too, which will be discussed in more detail in the following chapter of this essay.

[66] One could go on for ever, drawing examples as much from ancient as from more recent history. Among the most excessive and intrusive cases of exploitation to be recalled are the policy of Athenian democracy towards the allied cities; that of the Florentine democracy with respect to the surrounding countryside and to Pisa; and that of the democracies of the cantons of Berne, Uri, Schwyz and Unterwalden, with respect to the territories of Vaud and the Canton of Ticino.

[67] This naturally has not impeded England from making attacks of every kind, which do not have as *conditio sine qua non* the civilisation of the state, but the simple will to make particular interests prevail. It has however impeded the rise of imperialist sentiment, which sees in the state a higher entity whose rights extend as far as its might. England has created the greatest empire in the world but is at the same time, strange as it may seem, one of the countries least imbued with the mystical imperialist ethos.

[68] For the history of this particularly instructive experiment, see Arthur Rosenberg, *Geschichte der Deutschen Republik*, Karlsbad, Graphia, 1935. The difficulty which a democratic restoration has in getting the better of the traditions of the modern state depends on the specific necessity in which it finds itself to save institutions which are by no means republican in inspiration (which would see the activity of the state as a public service intended to satisfy the needs of the citizens), but imbued rather with a mystically imperialistic spirit (which permeates the activity of the state as an end to which the subjects must render their services).

The difficulty has however a much more general aspect. The deepest roots of the right of the state to demand the unconditional service of its citizens to satisfy its ends are found in the very consciousness of modern man: accustomed to such services, he recognises as an entirely natural thing the state's right to call him up for military service, battle and death. There have been entire epochs in which this power of obedience did not exist; but it is certain that the modern European state, whatever its social and political structure, as long as it has to reckon with the possibility of war, cannot start an education which allows that attitude to become obsolete but has to nourish it permanently in the heart of all its citizens. Therefore, even after a radical revolution, once the first dreams of a simple restriction are exhausted (unless there is a new international organisation which makes it impossible for the state to follow an imperialist line), there will re-emerge in the mind of the citizens, without substantial variations, the habitual consciousness of submission to the imperial requirements of the state. The relationship between state and subject returns to being as before. This may help explain how the French absolute monarchy re-emerged so quickly through the strengthened Napoleonic renown, and how the traditional Russian autocracy evolved into Stalinist centralisation. Even after the fall of the respective *anciens régimes*, the French and the Russians continued to feel themselves committed to give their lives for their respective states, unconditionally, and the objective circumstances did not allow a different consciousness to evolve.

[69] A good criticism of this theory is found in *The Economic Causes of War* by L. Robbins (New York, Macmillan, 1940), the reading of which is particularly recommended as an introduction to the study of the problems of the federal organisation of Europe.

[70] The words between quotation marks are those of Lenin himself. The piece is taken from the manifesto of the second congress of the Communist International of 1920 which, as is well-known, represents Lenin's most mature thinking on the world socialist revolution. The ideas on wartime state capitalism as a means of realising socialism were written during the war.

[71] The matter seems so obvious to them, that in the above-quoted manifesto, while the dictatorship of the proletariat is clearly seen as the taking into possession by part of the proletariat of the existing states, there is no explicit mention of the need to proceed to the formation of international political institutions. Only in passing, speaking not of the fate of large populations but of small ones, it is said that 'only the proletarian revolution can assure the small peoples of a free existence, by freeing the productive forces of all countries from the restrictions of the nation-states, and joining all peoples in compact economic cooperation, based on a general economic plan...'. The impossibility of making an international economic plan without having an international political power escapes the communists, usually so sensitive in appreciating the central importance of political power in all the doings of proletarian revolutions.

[72] The impossibility of making several sovereign socialist states coexist peacefully is identical to the impossibility of making several sovereign socialist communes coexist and cooperate. The communists have understood this second difficulty very well, have rejected communist-anarchic federalism and fought it when — in Spain — it threatened to dissolve everything into a powder of small factional and jealous communities. In the case of the coexistence of states, however, they assume instead the seraphic optimism of the anarchists, and are sure that everything will run to perfection unaided, without the need for

constraint by international law, as soon as the capitalist beast is destroyed. On the argument discussed in this paragraph, about the relations between independent socialist states, the fundamental work is: *Economic Planning and International Order* by L. Robbins (London, 1937), which gives a thorough account, from the economic point of view, of the theory of the need for the European federation.

[73] Actually there has been an attempt to see things from this point of view, and the incomprehension which it met with in the communist rank and file is significant. Trotsky, already during the first world war, was opposed to what he called Lenin's 'reverse nationalism' and had proposed to put on the agenda the socialist United States of Europe. In 1930 he wrote: 'The death knell tolled definitively for national programmes on the 14 August 1914. The revolutionary party of the proletariat cannot be based on anything but an international programme corresponding to the nature of the present age'. In 1931-32 he proposed a revolutionary plan for Germany, which at that time found itself on the brink of catastrophe. According to this plan, the central question must not be, as the communists however insisted, the establishment of a Soviet Germany, alongside Soviet Russia, but the union of the German and the Russian economies. He was perfectly aware however that the major obstacle to this line lay in Russian national socialism, which could not admit that it was in need of any integration from outside. In this incapacity of Russian national socialism to try to meet the crisis in the German economy, we see typical examples of the extreme difficulties of all kinds (such as that stemming from the need to review existing plans and to put everything into question again) which arise from the wish to achieve international socialism through national socialism. The two ways tend inevitably to diverge.

[74] Communists and socialists, proclaiming to be the sole depositories of the collectivist idea, refuse to take national-socialist collectivism seriously, and continue to speak of Germany as a capitalist country, because of the fact that the old capitalist managers have remained at the head of the various companies. But this only means that the Nazis have found it convenient to use the technical capacities of these people, and have been clever enough to succeed in so doing, leaving certain legal formalities in place. However, any industrial manager can be removed at a word from the government. The state establishes what is to be produced, determines the costs, fixes the selling prices and the entrepreneurs' emoluments (except, naturally, entrepreneurial fraud, which can happen however even in the communist type of collectivism). Briefly, it transforms them in fact into civil servants.

[75] Given the frequency with which demagogy exploits the absurd formula of the peoples' right to self-determination, to the point of separating from the state structure of which they form part, it is as well to emphasise that the admission of such a principle is irreconcilable with the very idea of federation. It would in fact transform it into a revived League of Nations, in which each state would still have, after suitably inflaming the national passions of its people, the right to refuse the common law, thus blowing up the whole edifice. The transfer of sovereignty to the federal state should necessarily be irrevocable.

[76] The federation would have another beneficial effect on movements for social renewal: an effect which can only be mentioned in a note. The socialist

movements have reached a dead end, not only because of the developments of militarist imperialism, but also because they are prisoners of their formula of collectivisation of the material means of production: a doomed formula, as has been shown both by scientific analysis and by practical experience. In order that the just demand of socialism — the emancipation of the working classes — should be met, there needs to be a revision of traditional ideas. This will enable a realisation of the limits of the advantages of collectivist measures, and of the fact that it is necessary to correct the ill effects of competition, but not to destroy it, since along with it would be eliminated the means for determining more rationally the utilisation of natural and human resources (cf. F. Hayek, *Collectivist Economic Planning*, London, 1935). The development of a socialist idea which justly values the function of free competition comes up against a huge weight of tradition as long as the general course of affairs, because of militarist requirements, is towards a growing collectivisation. In these circumstances, the line of least psychological resistance for socialists of all tendencies is to accept this way, demanding that it be used in favour of the working classes. The federation, by creating instead an atmosphere of free trade, naturally meets the process of working out more vital and fertile socialist ideas.

[77] Although it is not fashionable to include groups of workers among possible reactionary ranks, it has to be done. It is unlikely that in European countries, save for a few exceptional groups more deeply imbued with sectional egoism, there should be many workers who would support it very effectively. But this is not because there are not many who share in the profits of national restrictions, but because a European federation, while forcing many of them to change their occupation, would offer as a whole advantages so superior as to more than counterbalance the losses from the cessation of protectionism. Think however, to give a typical case, although not European, of the immense reactionary resistance that would be brought by the American working masses to a policy involving the abolition of immigration restrictions. Moreover, it should be borne in mind that the European workers are, in contrast to the Americans, too deeply imbued with progressive political ideologies to allow only those interests to prevail which would bring them to militate alongside the other classes in the reactionary camp. A typical case of ideal interests prevailing over material ones in the working classes can be seen in the support shown by the textile workers of Manchester for Lincoln's cause, when to follow their own economic interests they should have supported the anti-abolitionists of the south.

[78] To consider capitalism as a block whose interests are fairly homogeneous, and to limit these interests to the link existing between monopolistic capital and imperialist states, hinders socialist tendencies from objective consideration of the function that capitalist forces would have in a federal system, and makes them erroneously maintain that this system presupposes the abolition of capitalism. In reality, only a proportion of capitalists is linked to the destiny of the nation-states. On the other hand, the capitalist interests existing contrary to national autarkies (banks, export trade, producers of raw materials that can only find a sufficient outlet in a world market, producers that use foreign raw materials, etc.) are notably important. This mass of interests would grow rapidly in the direction of capitalism taken as a whole, as soon as the federal system was established. The task of transforming anaemic autarkic markets into a single rich continental

market would fall substantially to them. Without the support of this free trade capitalism with its unifying force, the federation would find itself obliged to resolve the superhuman problem of unifying the *membra disiecta* of the individual national economies by bureaucratic means.

[79] It is particularly worth noting the *Lettere politiche* by Junius published in Italy in the *Corriere della Sera* of 1918-19 and reprinted in 1920 (Bari, Laterza). The seventh and ninth letters still deserve reflection today. (Editor's note: Junius was the pseudonym used by Luigi Einaudi who, after World War Two, became the first President of the Italian Republic. See p. 4 above.)

[80] People of good sense foresaw, even before it was set up, the absolute ineffectiveness of the League of Nations, with its respect for the complete sovereignty of the individual states. Apart from the aforementioned letters of Junius, see for example the biting judgement of Winston Churchill, who formed part of the British delegation to Versailles (cf. the note to page 232 of *Guerra diplomatica* by Aldovrandi Marescotti, Milan, 1939).

Index

Acton, Lord 3

Adams, John viii

America, United States of (USA)
24, 25, 27, 35, 37, 38, 54, 58, 59, 60, 63, 77, 78, 81

Asia 76, 81

Attlee, Clement 13

Australia 24, 25

Austria 39

Balkans 81

Beethoven, Ludwig van 67

Belgium 17, 24

Benelux 13

Bentham, Jeremy 50

Beveridge, Lord (William) 3, 4, 5, 6, 9, 17, 18, 45, 46, 69

Bismarck, Otto von 54, 55

Blum, Léon 23, 79

Britain, Great (UK)
iii, 1, 2, 4, 5, 11, 12, 16, 17, 19, 21, 22, 23, 24, 25, 26, 27, 31, 34,

38, 41, 54, 55, 77, 81

Bryce, James 3

Caligula 59

Canada 24, 25, 26

Cannan, Edwin 45

Carr, E.H. 34

China 37, 77

Churchill, Sir Winston 17

Cobden, Richard 55, 61, 100

Comintern 22

Commonwealth, British 25, 41

Community, European vii, 4, 5, 8, 10, 13, 14, 15, 16, 69, 70

Croce, Benedetto 2

Czechoslovakia 20, 25, 39

Daladier, Edouard 23

De Gasperi, Alcide 13

Denmark 24

Dominions, British 25, 26, 36

Eckhart, Meister 107

Einaudi, Luigi 2, 3, 6, 69

England 35

Finland 24

Foch, Maréchal Ferdinand 20, 22

France 2, 12, 13, 17, 22, 23, 24, 38, 41, 94

Franklin, Benjamin viii

Frederick William, King of Prussia 54

Freud, Sigmund 103

Germany
4, 6, 8, 9, 12, 13, 17, 19, 21, 22, 23, 24, 25, 35, 36, 38, 39, 42, 46,

54, 55, 67, 70, 76, 77, 78, 80, 89, 94, 95, 106, 115, 116

Hamilton, Alexander viii, 13, 58, 64, 65

Hayek, Friedrich von 5, 6, 17

Hitler, Adolf 23, 55, 80

Hume, David 50

India 26

Ireland 24, 25, 81

Italy 1, 7, 8, 12, 13, 16, 35, 37, 70, 76

Japan 37, 76, 77

Jay, John viii, 13

Jefferson, Thomas viii

Jennings, Ivor vii, 5, 17

Kant, Immanuel 2

Karoly, Mihaly 79

Laski, Harold vii, 17

Layton, Walter 3

League of Nations 32, 33, 34, 58, 65, 80, 97, 116

Lenin, Vladimir Ilyich 55

Lincoln, Abraham 60, 64

List, Friedrich 54

Lloyd George, David 20

Lothian, Lord (Philip Kerr) vii, 5

Mackay, Kim vii

Mackay, R.W.G. 12, 13

Madison, James viii, 13, 65

Marshall, T.E. 2

Marx, Karl 55, 99, 100

Mazzini, Giuseppe 4

Meade, James 5, 17

Michelangelo, Simone Buonarotti 67

Mitterrand, François 15, 70

Monnet, Jean vii, 13, 14, 15, 16, 69

Mussolini, Benito 1, 69, 70

Negrin, Juan 79

Netherlands, The 17, 24

New Zealand 25

Newton, Sir Isaac 67

Norway 24

Pascal, Blaise 67

Poland 20, 25, 39

Portugal 35

Proudhon, Pierre-Joseph 4

Rappard, William 46

Rembrandt van Rijn, Harmenszoon 67

Ricardo, David 54

Robbins, Lord (Lionel) vii, 3, 4, 5, 6, 10, 17, 45, 46, 47, 69

Rossi, Ernesto 2, 3, 6, 10, 11, 69, 70, 71

Roumania 21

Russia 7, 22, 35, 37, 42, 79

Schmoller, Gustav von 54

Scotland 35

Seeley, Sir John 3

Shakespeare, William 67

Sidgwick, Henry 3

Smith, Adam 50, 52, 53, 54, 55

Socrates 67

South Africa 25, 26

Soviet Union (USSR) 2, 8, 22, 25

Spaak, Paul-Henri 13

Spain 35

Spinelli, Altiero
viii, 1, 2, 3, 4, 5, 6, 7, 8, 9, 10, 11, 12, 13, 14, 15, 16, 46, 69,

70, 71

Spinoza, Benedict de 67

Streit, Clarence 28

Sweden 24

Switzerland 24

Thatcher, Baroness (Margaret) 4

Toynbee, Arnold vii

Turkey 35

Union, European viii, 1, 4, 15, 16, 70

Washington, George viii

Wheare, Kenneth vii, 5, 17

Wilson, Lord (Harold) 5, 17

Wootton, Barbara vii, 3, 5, 17